Praise for *Starting Strong*

"Whether seeking to strengthen your own mentoring practice, administer a mentoring program within your organization, or develop your ability to 'tune in' to others and navigate candid conversations—*Starting Strong* provides a unique avenue to help mentors and mentees become more reflective, observant, and introspective—to allow them to grow into the type of professionals they wish to become."

—Peg McCue Guillon, chairperson,
MetLife Legal Affairs Mentoring Program

"Remarkable! One of the finest books I have read on mentoring, this accessible and practical book reads like a novel, and rings with the reality of the business world even as it brilliantly moves us deep inside the mentoring relationship at its best. Zachary and Fischler both entertain and instruct us as we watch how a savvy yet very human mentor works with an earnest younger protégé, artfully ripening the relationship into the kind of respect and affection that characterizes a powerful mentoring experience. For anyone wanting to learn more or teach others about how mentors can make a difference in real peoples' lives, this trove of practical advice and genuine wisdom is pure gold."

—Laurent A. Parks Daloz, Senior Fellow,
Whidbey Institute, and author of *Mentor: Guiding
the Journey of Adult Learners*

"In this strikingly engaging book, Zachary and Fischler focus on one of the most important dynamics in mentoring: how trust is established at the beginning of the relationship. The story of Rafa and Cynthia is one of bumps and affirmations, growing understanding, and the conjunction of ambition and experience. Through a series of conversations that show the ways listening and questioning work to deepen communication, *Starting Strong* takes us to the heart of what it means to be a mentor."

—Stephen Brookfield, John Ireland Endowed Chair,
University of St. Thomas, Minneapolis-St. Paul

"Congratulations, you have a mentor (or mentee)! Now what? Instead of winging it, hoping for the best, you can now structure the relationship right from the beginning to make it a satisfying experience for both of you. Part fable, part guidebook, part manual, the authors have highlighted the keys to success for a rich mentor-mentee partnership. *Starting Strong* is not to be missed by anyone open to this life-changing partnership."

—Marshall Goldsmith, author of the *New York Times*
and global bestseller *What Got You Here Won't Get You There*

Starting Strong

A Mentoring Fable

Lois J. Zachary, Lory A. Fischler

Strategies for Success in the First 90 Days

JB JOSSEY-BASS™
A Wiley Brand

Copyright © 2014 by John Wiley & Sons, Inc. All rights reserved.
Published by Jossey-Bass
A Wiley Brand
One Montgomery Street, Suite 1200, San Francisco, CA 94104-4594
www.josseybass.com/highereducation

Jossey-Bass books and products are available through most bookstores. To contact Jossey-Bass directly call our Customer Care Department within the U.S. at 800-956-7739, outside the U.S. at 317-572-3986, or fax 317-572-4002.

Wiley publishes in a variety of print and electronic formats and by print-on-demand. Some material included with standard print versions of this book may not be included in e-books or in print-on-demand. If this book refers to media such as a CD or DVD that is not included in the version you purchased, you may download this material at http://booksupport.wiley.com. For more information about Wiley products, visit www.wiley.com.

Library of Congress Cataloging-in-Publication Data
Zachary, Lois J.
   Starting strong : a mentoring fable / Lois J. Zachary, Lory A. Fischler.
      pages   cm
   Includes bibliographical references and index.
   ISBN 978-1-118-76771-9 (hardback); 978-1-118-76790-0 (ebk.);
   978-1-118-76805-1 (ebk.)
      1. Mentoring in business.   2. Corporate culture.   I. Fischler, Lory A., 1947-
II. Title.
   HF5385.Z334   2014
   658.3'124—dc23

                                                                    2014013596

Printed in the United States of America
FIRST EDITION
HB Printing   10 9 8 7 6 5 4 3 2 1

Contents

Foreword

In *Starting Strong*, Lois Zachary and her colleague, Lory Fischler, craft a memorable fable that takes us inside and alongside a mentoring relationship as it plays out over time. We find ourselves listening in on the conversations and learning firsthand about the issues a mentor and mentee experience at the start of their relationship.

The story these authors relate focuses on the evolution of one particular relationship. Yet, its characters, conversations, and context are familiar enough that they will be recognized by anyone who has been in a mentoring relationship or has been charged with supporting mentors and mentees.

I am a great believer that the continuing learning conversations that take place over time are the core of a mentoring relationship. In the most effective mentoring relationships, there are many learning conversations: one in the head of the mentor and mentee before they meet; one after they meet, reflecting on the conversation and the learning to be taken from it; the spoken conversation during the mentoring meeting; and the unspoken, silent conversation in the heads of mentor and mentee as they converse. Zachary and Fischler expose all these conversations. Experienced mentors, like the one in this fable, continuously work at honing this skill.

The mentor and mentee in this fable are both keen to establish a clear sense of direction in their early conversations. They cast this purposeful activity in the language of goals because this is part of the managerial culture and education. We know that setting goals that are too specific at the beginning can be detrimental to the quality of the relationship, causing it to focus on narrow, transactional outcomes. It gets in the way of one of the most powerful processes of effective mentoring—the gradual emergence and flowering of deeper goals, more closely aligned to the mentee's personal values and energy. The mentor and mentee in this relationship do get to SMART goals, but only when the mentee is far enough along the path of understanding himself and his career purpose.

The mentor is very specific about what she will and won't do on behalf of the mentee and makes it very clear from the start that her mentee must take responsibility for his own learning. When the mentor gives advice, it is timely and designed to provide context, so that the mentee can make up his own mind about what to do and how to apply it.

Successful mentoring relationships tend to involve periodic reviews of the relationship itself. What would we each like the other to do more or less of? Do we want to broaden or deepen the issues we explore? How can we be more honest with each other? What needs to change as the mentee's knowledge (wisdom) grows and he becomes more aware of his inner and external environments? We see in this fable how the very act of asking questions like these enhances the mutual respect and trust between mentor and mentee and stimulates their conversations that deliver even greater value.

Stories, like this one have the power to capture our imagination in a way that textbooks can't. Each mentoring relationship is a learning journey, in the tradition of the "hero's journey"—a voyage into the unknown, meeting challenges and conquering fears, and gradually learning to know and respect oneself. Homer (the ancient Greek, not Simpson) would have approved of the lessons learned from Zachary and Fischler's fable!

David Clutterbuck
Maidenhead, Berkshire, UK

Introduction

Plato said it first: "The beginning is the most important part of the work." He wasn't talking about mentoring, but he might as well have been.

Mentoring success depends on a strong beginning—the crucial first ninety days, when mentors and mentees, new to working together as mentoring partners, must build trust and lay the groundwork for realizing the full potential of the relationship. It is a critical time that sets the tone, direction, energy, and momentum for mentoring success. In *Starting Strong*, we invite you to sit in on the first three months of a brand-new mentoring relationship and observe it as it unfolds.

What do really good mentors do to make a difference?

How do they engage their mentees, create good conversation, and keep it going?

How do mentor and mentee move past the idea of "advice" and into a trust-based relationship that generates real learning?

These questions were top of mind as we wrote this fable. Whether you are a new or experienced mentor, or a newly minted mentee, we encourage you to listen to the conversations and the inner thoughts of this mentor-mentee partnership as they work together to build their relationship.

Cynthia, the mentor, is a savvy and seasoned marketing executive, supervisor, and experienced mentor. She is well grounded in effective mentoring techniques, and she looks to learn something from every new relationship.

Rafa, the new mentee, is a young and ambitious former athlete turned financial analyst. He is unsure of what mentoring really means and what the process might be, but he hopes that mentoring will set him on the path to becoming a company superstar. The framework, obstacles, and successes of the mentoring process for both partners are revealed as their relationship grows and transforms through their conversations, challenges, laughter, and breakthroughs.

If you recognize elements of yourself or your coworkers in these characters, that's because our fable is based very firmly in reality: Cynthia and Rafa are composites drawn from actual people. Their issues are based on those of the many mentors and mentees we have worked with, interviewed, and coached over the past decade, and their work together is authentic.

How to Use This Book

We have divided *Starting Strong* into two parts: Part One, The Fable, and Part Two, The Mentoring Conversation Playbook. Our fable follows one mentoring partnership, but it offers tools and skills that can be applied to any mentoring relationship in any setting. The Conversation Playbook is a quick guide to establishing a trust-based relationship and keeping it strong.

What You'll Find in the Fable

The Fable takes you inside the relationship in real time, as it is taking place. You'll be privy not only to Cynthia and Rafa's conversations, but also to their inner thoughts about the process.

Each chapter in the Fable focuses on a particular mentoring meeting, and the chapter subtitles characterize the essence of the conversation that needs to take place. The Week Before is an email exchange that takes place before Cynthia and Rafa meet for the first time. In the First Meeting, the mentoring partners spend time getting to know each other and building the relationship. The Second Meeting focuses on conversations that establish mentoring agreements between them. The Third and Fourth Meetings highlight conversations about goal setting, taking Rafa's starter goals and converting them into smarter goals. In the Fifth Meeting, Cynthia and Rafa encounter a stumbling block that they must address before they can move on. The Sixth Meeting takes place at the ninety-day mark, when Rafa and Cynthia check in on their overall progress. Finally, the Epilogue jumps forward five years, revealing what the future held in store for Cynthia and Rafa, and how their mentoring process played out over the long term.

In anticipation of readers who are looking to dig deeper, we've prepared a series of questions at the end of each chapter to help you integrate the lessons embedded in this fable and apply them to your current mentoring relationships. You can use the questions to trigger deeper understanding, to engage in conversation with your mentoring partner, or as a guide for group conversation. Whether you are preparing to embark on a mentoring relationship, just starting out, looking to improve a mentoring relationship, or reflecting on past mentoring experiences, these questions should help take you to the next level. You may choose to address the questions as you read through the Fable, or leave them until you are finished with the book, or even return to them later in the course of your own mentoring experiences. Ultimately, we hope they will stimulate your thinking and lead to more reflective mentoring practice.

If you are a new mentor, you will find it helpful to keep Cynthia's tips (at the end of the Fable) in mind as you launch your own relationship. Think about how they might impact and influence your own approach. If you are an experienced mentor, you may find Cynthia's tips useful as a way of evaluating your current mentoring practice. Ask yourself if any of her strategies might improve your own outcomes. For mentees, they provide a snapshot of good mentor practice.

Mentees can benefit from the tips Rafa provides at the end of the Fable. Rafa was also new to the mentoring relationship, so his tips can help you prepare yourself more effectively for what is to come. If you are a mentor, you may also want to glance at them to refresh your understanding of what it's like to be on the other side of the relationship.

What You'll Find in the Conversation Playbook

Part Two, The Mentoring Conversation Playbook, is a handy reference to specific strategies that underlie effective mentoring. We highlight six essential conversations you will want to have in the first ninety days—the ones you've read in the six chapters of the Fable. In this section we go deeper, offering strategies that enhance mentoring success and a set of probing questions you can use to deepen your discussion. At the end of each essential conversation you will find a readiness check-in to prepare you to move forward with your mentoring partner.

The resources in the Conversation Playbook are designed to be just that—an aid, not a script. Each relationship is different, as is each mentor and mentee. If you are experienced in mentoring, tap into the strategies that best enhance what you already do. If you are new to mentoring, use the Playbook as a way to familiarize yourself with the processes and topics that contribute to building trust, setting the stage, focusing on learning, and engaging the mentee. Mentees may find the probing questions useful as a preparation or reflection tool.

A Personal Invitation to Mentoring

Whether you are new to mentoring or already highly committed to a mentoring relationship, we encourage you to read the Fable from start to finish first. Feel the rhythm of the relationship before you turn to the Playbook for the details.

The mentoring partnership grows in the fertile soil of good conversation, in which mentors skillfully and thoughtfully use conversation to help their mentees probe their own thinking and discover answers for themselves. The mentor's ability to do this isn't magic; it's grounded in a practical understanding of the levels of conversation and what it takes to move from level to level—strategies you will learn in this Playbook.

If you are about to embark on your mentoring relationship, we suggest that you and your mentoring partner review the questions and strategies in Part Two together. Decide jointly which strategies and probing questions might enrich your mentoring conversations, strengthen your relationship, and accelerate learning.

A few caveats. First, if you are a mentor, model Cynthia, but don't try to imitate her: be authentic and true to your own style. Experienced mentors should look for ways to improve on what they do. This book provides some clear examples. Although we believe there are predictable phases and processes that all mentoring relationships need to address, they must always take a back seat to the immediate needs and concerns of the mentee. Don't move forward until your mentee is ready.

We hope Cynthia and Rafa's mentoring journey will generate insights that resonate for you on many levels. Perhaps your self-awareness will increase as you recognize yourself in the narrative; perhaps you will be able to identify what is missing in your personal mentoring practice. Rafa and Cynthia's conversations may spark some new ideas for you, suggesting new behaviors, skills, and techniques to add to your mentoring toolkit.

There's one thing we know from our own experience: no matter how many times you've been a mentor, you can always get better. One of the ways to get better is by reflecting on practice—your own and others'. This fable is our personal invitation to you to deepen your understanding of mentoring, further your own growth and development, and add value to your personal mentoring relationships by starting strong.

—*Lois Zachary and Lory Fischler*

Starting Strong

Part One

The Fable

The Week Before:
Questions Before We Start

From: Cynthia Colton <cynthia.colton@CTBN.biz>
Subject: Introducing myself
To: Rafa Moretti <rafa.moretti@CTBN.biz>

Rafa,

Diane Foster's email announcing our mentoring match just arrived. I am looking forward to meeting you in person. In the meantime, I thought it might be helpful if I provided a little background information in addition to what you've probably already seen on the website. My purpose is to help you understand why I am so committed to mentoring

I'm a Chicago native, and I attended Northwestern as an undergraduate majoring in journalism. I worked as an intern at the Trib and then got hired on right after graduation. I was in love with the idea of being an ace reporter, and sure that it was the only career for me. Well, it took a couple of years of floundering—it was hard to let go of my dream. Finally, I realized that this was NOT my ideal job. I needed to be in a position where I could create the action and not just report on it. For a while, I was at a loss about what to do next.

People always say that for every door that closes, one opens, and that's exactly what happened to me. I was introduced to Frank Tibbitz by a good friend, and we hit it off. Frank helped me realize how much I needed to understand what was really motivating me. At that time, he was a VP of Marketing & Communications. It was an area that interested me but which I didn't know much about. I owe him a big debt of gratitude for pointing me in the right direction and helping me stay on track. Frank has been one of my mentors ever since.

I made two big decisions right away: I went back to school in communications, and I took a job as a marketing research analyst. I moved on to become an internal communications manager and then a marketing communications coordinator at Carmel in Boston. Twelve years ago I moved to New York City and took a position as Global Communications Manager for BeST, where I spent more time in the air than on the ground. It was exciting, but the cold weather finally got to me. So here I am at CTBN in Phoenix, holding a position with the same job title as Frank—VP of Marketing and Communications. Who knew!

Frank wasn't my first mentor, and he certainly wasn't my last. At first, mentors were assigned to me as part of my leadership training. And then I searched for my own mentors. Each raised the bar for me, challenged my thinking, and supported my development. Even though I have moved on, I still hear their voices resonating in my head when I walk into a meeting or find myself in a difficult situation. All of them have contributed to my growth and professional development as a leader. I can honestly say that I wouldn't be where I am today without them.

You can see that I truly believe in the power of mentoring! I make it a priority to mentor others, no matter how much work I have on my plate. I believe it is part of my responsibility as a leader. The best part is that I continue to learn from each and every one of my mentees. It's a real two-way relationship.

Rafa, I am looking forward to learning more about you. I have prepared some questions to speed the process along and help me get to know you a little better before our first meeting.

1. How did you get to CTBN?

2. What are your career aspirations?

3. What do you see as your strengths and challenges?

4. How do you let off steam?

5. Why did you choose me as your mentor?

6. What would you like me to know about you?

If you can respond in the next couple of days, it will help us make the most of our time together. Thanks. I am looking forward to connecting in real time on Friday.

Best regards,
Cynthia
Cynthia Colton, MBA
www.ctbn.biz

―――――――

From: Rafa Moretti <rafa.moretti@CTBN.biz>
Subject: Re: Introducing myself
To: Cynthia Colton <cynthia.colton@CTBN.biz>

Hi Cynthia!
Thanks for your note. I'm really excited about this. We already have some things in common. You spent some time in the city I was raised in—Boston—and I also had a bit of a career jolt.

I spent every single day since I was eight years old working towards a career as a professional baseball player. I was actually a pretty good shortstop, which led to a free ride to Milton Academy during high school (that would never have been in the cards for a kid like me from the North End). I batted .395 for four years. I am pretty proud that they retired my number when I graduated. My parents didn't care about my batting average, though; they only cared about my grade point average. As long as I made Headmaster's List, they were OK. Thank goodness I did.

Remember the movie "Blind Side"? At the end of movie all the college coaches came knocking at this talented high school football star's door to recruit him. That was me—only smarter and a baseball player. I was heavily recruited by colleges all across the country but chose Boston College. It made for an easier move and my parents were pushing the Jesuits. I was totally focused on getting drafted and playing in the majors. No other goal was remotely possible.

So, kind of like you, the door slammed in my face. In my junior year a runner slid into second base during a double play. I held the ball and got the out, but his cleats ruptured my Achilles tendon. Unfortunately, I returned too quickly to practice and reinjured it, and was told it was never going to be right. It hurt like hell both times, but not nearly as badly as the loss of my dream. That was almost 6 years ago.

You asked me to respond to your 6 questions. So here goes.

How did I get to CTBN?

Every summer for most of my life I was in some kind of baseball program. But the summer of my junior year, bored out of my mind and hobbling on crutches, I needed to do something else. Then a door opened that I never expected. One of the booster club members, a senior VP at McCowen's, got me an internship working in supply chain management. I was surprised how much I liked being in a business that had nothing to do with swinging a bat. I actually enjoyed analyzing numbers on a page and deciphering them so they made sense to other people. It was hard to let go of a lifelong dream, but maybe my discipline from sports helped—I put the same energy I used to put into training to set a new career direction. Anyway, I graduated BC with a business degree and I took a job with CD Worth as a financial analyst.

About two years ago, a former teammate (Jack Fallon, he works in sales) called to tell me about a job opening here. It was for more money, which didn't hurt. Plus, the draw of watching pro ball teams do spring training in the Cactus League in Phoenix was very appealing. I had never participated in any formal leadership training, so I was psyched when I heard about the CTBN NextGen Leadership Program.

What are my career aspirations?

I always try to do things to the best of my ability. I have no tolerance for mediocrity in my team or myself. I learned that from baseball. I've never been afraid of hard work. I do what it takes to win, and I expect others to do the same. So down the road, I am hoping that my skills and talent will be recognized by senior leadership. I want a place in this organization where I can advance and make an impact!!

What are my strengths and challenges?

My strengths—I take on a leadership role in whatever I do. On the baseball field or wherever, I push for best effort from everyone. I am not afraid of a challenge, and not afraid to fight for an issue I believe in. I go for results and cut through the BS. I can put in a long day and get a lot done. And I can still hit a fastball deep into center field. ☺

My challenges—Like everyone, I have my challenges. I struggle with people who sit around and complain about a problem rather than work on the solution. I get frustrated with people who aren't getting the results they need, but won't ask for help or try a new approach. I also get frustrated when leaders keep doing the same thing, using old systems and technology. It keeps us from being efficient and competitive, even though they don't seem to care. It sets us up for losing and that is really intolerable for me.

How do I let off steam?

I still play a little ball on Saturdays in a men's league—nothing serious. Can't completely let go of baseball. ☺ I also work out regularly, and I am in the gym, pumping iron.

Why did I choose you?

When I was asked to submit three names of potential mentors, your name came to mind immediately. I watched you present at the Ops meeting last spring and I was very impressed. You have made a big mark on CTBN, and everyone respects you. You reminded me of what it felt like to be up at the plate, bottom of the ninth, bases loaded, with everything on the line. The crowd expects big things from you, and you deliver a walk-off run. I am hoping to be in a job someday where I can have the same power and influence that you do.

What would I like you to know about me?

I am not sure there is more to tell, but I will summarize by saying I am hard working, interested in learning and getting ahead. I want to be able to make a contribution to any organization I am with, and I hope that organization wants me to make a difference too.

Meeting with you is a great start. I look forward to Friday.

Regards,

Rafa

Digging Deeper

Questions for Mentors:

1. Cynthia sent an email to Rafa to introduce herself. What is the value of sending an introductory letter or email in advance of meeting? Is there a downside?

2. What did you like about Cynthia's email? Is there anything you didn't like in Cynthia's letter?

3. What information would you include in your own letter?

4. Did Cynthia share more, less, or about the same amount of personal information that you might share with your mentee?

5. Cynthia included six questions at the end of her email to Rafa. What is the advantage of including specific questions?

6. What questions might you want to ask your mentee?

Questions for Mentees:

1. Cynthia sent an email to her mentee to introduce herself. What is the value in receiving an introductory letter or email in advance of meeting? Do you see any downside?

2. What did you like about Cynthia's email to Rafa? What more would you have wanted to know after reading it?

3. Is there anything that Rafa shared in his email to Cynthia that you would delete or change?

4. What information would you include in a email to your mentor?

5. Did Rafa share more, less, or about the same amount of personal information that you might share with your mentor?

6. Cynthia included six questions at the end of her email to Rafa. How comfortable would you be responding to her questions? Were there any other questions you would have wished she had asked?

7. What questions would you want to ask your mentor to get to know him better?

The First Meeting: Powering Up

A bad accident on the 101 at 7:30 A.M. had backed up traffic for miles. At this rate, Cynthia wasn't sure she would get through it in time for her first meeting with Rafa, her new mentee. Rescheduling certainly wouldn't make for a good start to the relationship. She pounded the wheel with her fists. *I hate being late!* Realizing there was nothing she could do, she sighed, settled back in her seat, and began thinking about the relationship she was about to begin with Rafa. *I might as well use this time for something productive.*

Cynthia liked what she had seen in Rafa's email: his easy style and his wry humor. His direct way of responding to her questions intrigued her and offered some insight into his personality. He had portrayed himself as ambitious, focused, high-energy, competitive, and driven. Those were all good qualities for a career in business. He certainly had an unusual background, one she'd not seen before. He was young, just five years out of college. In some respects he reminded of her eighteen-year-old son, Jason; he loved baseball too, but not as a career choice, thank goodness—Cynthia had a fair idea of how few of those who aspire to the life of a professional athlete ever realize their dream.

She reflected on her strategy for their meeting. Her first priority was to put Rafa at ease and to earn his trust. She wanted to get to know him quickly, so she mentally rehearsed some questions she wanted to ask: Why had he chosen baseball over some other sport? How had his injury affected him? Who are the people who influenced him the most? Has he ever had a mentor? Does he really know what mentoring is? She certainly didn't when her own career began . . . Just as her thoughts began drifting to her own experience, traffic started moving, and she pressed her foot down on the accelerator. They must have cleared that accident. She'd be only a few minutes late after all.

———————

Rafa sat outside Cynthia's office feeling nervous, just as he always had on opening day. Even his palms were sweaty. *Great.* He took a few deep breaths and tried to relax, but relaxation wasn't coming easily. He'd arrived a little early, but Cynthia was late.

His thoughts wandered to the NextGen Leadership Program he'd just completed. He had been excited and flattered when he was chosen to participate—he knew that they asked only those employees they thought showed leadership potential. NextGen had come at the ideal time for him, a year after he was first hired on and just as he was getting antsy and bored with his job. It had been a good experience and was a real motivator for him. It had rekindled the spark. He was more eager than ever to advance his career, and he knew he needed help to do that.

The mentoring component was the final piece of the NextGen program, and everyone said he'd really lucked out being matched with Cynthia as his mentor. She was one of the most admired and respected leaders in the company. Right out of the gate she had repositioned CTBN'S entire marketing approach, much to the disappointment of the old guard. But despite their moaning, she'd persevered. Her critics eventually left the company; a couple were asked to leave. Within a few months she was named a vice president. Rafa gave her a mental high five. Cynthia was everything Rafa aspired to be as a leader: admired, respected, and influential, a go-getter, a visionary, and a change agent. So where was she? He looked at his watch. She was actually only a minute late. He must have been really early.

Rafa wondered how easy it would be to talk to her. She had a reputation for pushing until she got the results she wanted, and word had it that she didn't suffer fools. He wanted to start off on the right foot and get her on his side—to have her believe in him and see his potential. As he waited, emailer's remorse began to set in. Had he given her the kind of answers she was looking for? Had he said enough about his strengths and abilities? Had he said too much? *Dude, why did you use those emoticons? What if we don't click? What if she thinks I'm not worthy of her time and effort?*

"Rafa? Hello, so good to meet you. Sorry I'm late. Traffic!" Cynthia extended her hand for a strong, welcoming handshake, wrangling her large tote bag at the same time. "Come on in, let me put this down, and we can get started." She smiled and opened the door to her office.

Rafa rushed to hold the door for her, smiling in return, and in relief. She seemed nice. "It's great to meet you too, I've been looking forward to this meeting. I really appreciated your letter and your very quick response. A couple of people in my leadership cohort are still waiting to hear from their mentors. I feel lucky."

Cynthia chuckled. "Oh, lucky! Lucky that I responded so quickly? Or lucky to have me as a mentor?

Her laugh was contagious. "Both, naturally," he said. "No, really, I did appreciate hearing from you so quickly. I mean, like having a mentor who is, like, so senior in the organization . . ." *Stop babbling!* "And, oh, I appreciated you telling me about your background and some of the disappointments you faced in your own career."

She sat down at a table and motioned him to sit in the chair across from him. Rafa looked around the room, a window office with an amazing view. The pictures on the wall caught his eye—he recognized many familiar faces, mostly local and national names in the news. He loved the shot of her at a Chicago Bulls game standing alongside Michael Jordan and Scottie Pippen. There were framed certificates and awards that she had received for her expertise in marketing, including an obviously prestigious leadership award for strategic communication and a statuette from a local nonprofit.

Pictures of her two children at various ages sat on the shelf behind her desk. What really captured his attention, though, was the framed quote next to them: "Seek first to understand, then to be understood." *She must be the real deal, that's for sure.*

"You've had a pretty interesting career path," he said with clear admiration.

Cynthia shrugged off the compliment. "You've had a very interesting journey yourself, especially for someone so young."

She leaned toward him, steering the conversation to the topic of Boston, an interest they had in common. They spent the next few minutes chatting easily about the city's hot spots and comparing their favorite seafood restaurants. Eventually, the conversation turned to the rivalry between the Red Sox and the Yankees. It gave Cynthia the opening she was looking for. "I see that baseball has been a big influence in your life. What got you into it? How come it has been such a passion?"

"Well, I'm a natural athlete, and there were lots of sports I could have chosen," Rafa responded. "For a while I was torn between soccer and baseball. But my grandfather and I used to go to Fenway together all the time. Have you ever seen the movie *Field of Dreams?*"

She smiled. "Funny you should mention that movie. On my last plane trip across country I just happened to watch it—for about the tenth time. I love the scene with Kevin Costner and James Earl Jones at the Red Sox game. So, which one were you? Costner or Jones?"

"Neither. But that movie really, really spoke to me. You know, how Costner loved baseball so much. It made me see the elegance of the game. And the line 'Go the distance'—well, it's become kind of a mantra for me. But the scene at Fenway—that's where I made my decision to drop soccer and play ball."

Cynthia shook her head. "You know, I never did get inside Fenway Park the whole time I was in Boston. That, I regret. I loved the line, 'If you build it, they will come.' Classic marketing line!"

Rafa laughed, nodding his head. "Yeah, never thought about that. It's true! That movie had so many great lines. 'Ease his pain.' Little did I know how much I'd need to draw on that one later."

Cynthia paused before she spoke again. "You were awfully young to have to deal with such a traumatic injury. It couldn't have been easy for you."

Rafa stared back at her blankly and she waited for his response. He waited too, hoping that Cynthia would drop the subject. But he could see she wanted something from him. Reluctantly, he said, "Well, let's just say I wouldn't want to go through that again."

"So, what got you through it?"

"Hmmm. What got me through it? I never really thought whether there was an 'it.' Every serious competitive athlete knows there are going to be injuries. You're going to get hurt at some point. I'd been hurt before. Most of the time it's just ice and ibuprofen. Occasionally, you sit out and take a rest. Which is what I did. That's what I always had to deal with in the past. For a while, I rehabbed. That was my focus: Go the distance. Ease his pain. That's what I drew on. It never occurred to me that it would be permanent. Not once." He paused, his smile gone for a moment; then it returned.

"So for six months I focused on getting better. That gave me a goal. And then I could see it wasn't going to happen. And then it was clear that I was done. What got me through that? I guess I haven't really thought about that. The first solution to every problem in my family is to eat. So my mom immediately started cooking!" He laughed. "I gained twelve pounds on her lasagna."

Cynthia was nodding, clearly paying attention.

She's taking this pretty seriously. Rafa adjusted his tone. "Yeah, I never really thought about it. That was a really rough time for me. My whole life was playing ball. My friends were my teammates and my roommates. Life was all about baseball and all about playing, and I mean *all*. When baseball went away, it became too hard to hang out and just watch everyone else suit up and play. I didn't even want to leave my room. Yeah, I guess I was probably pretty depressed for about eight months . . ."

"So," Cynthia said, "besides your mom's great dinners, what got you through it?"

"Well, my dad kept shooting me these looks like, 'When you going to stop feeling so sorry for yourself and get your butt moving again?' And then I guess . . . huh, I guess the same discipline I used when I played ball just automatically kicked in. First, I focused all my energy on getting off crutches and walking without a limp. And then getting stronger, and then being able to run. The running helped. I had time to myself, and my mind wandered constantly. And then, on one of my workouts, it came to me. I needed to find something else to get excited about. I realized that what worked for me getting good at baseball could be applied to a career I could be successful at. That I could still be part of a team and contribute to winning. I felt like I had a future again. I guess that's how I got through it. And then one day I woke up and realized that I actually liked working with numbers. Weird, huh?"

"Is that what led you to the financial analyst job?"

"I guess so. In baseball, you rely on your statistics and numbers to tell you exactly how you're doing and to improve your game. Like, swinging at the first pitch was never a good idea for me. My batting average dropped when I swung too early or when I went after pitches that were low and away. The stats showed me that those were my weakness. I raised my average when I learned to be patient and swing at the right pitch. Now that I'm an FA I use the same discipline and number analysis to drive business results for the company."

The more she listened, the more Cynthia found herself caught up by his story. She could feel his pain. Rafa's determination and focus were clearly key drivers for him. She liked hearing that he recognized his strengths and used them as he transitioned to a new career, and she told him so.

"Thanks, Cynthia. I'm not sure where I would be if I hadn't made the link."

Cynthia leaned back in her chair and crossed her arms. "I know what it is to feel a sense of loss and then to have to struggle to find something else to replace a dream."

"You mean your career in journalism?"

"Yes. Like you, I always assumed there was only one future for me—being a reporter."

"I don't quite understand how you made the jump from journalism to marketing and communications. I know your mentor had something to do with it."

"That's right. Frank Tibbitz was a family friend of one of my old friends who knew I was struggling. He'd read some of my articles in the *Trib*, and he thought I was pretty good, and when we met we just hit it off. It wasn't any kind of formal program, but he'd learned a lot in his own career and enjoyed sharing the wealth. We talked about my talent for writing, and he thought I should probably be looking for a new field where I could use it in some way. So he gave me an assignment—to identify a list of careers that required skilled writing. His assignment took some work, and later I realized that his assignment had forced me to expand my thinking."

As Rafa listened to her story, he started to relax, getting into it and forgetting himself.

She continued, "All that research stimulated my curiosity. For the first time, I was actually doing something proactively to build a career for myself. I stopped feeling sorry for myself for 'failing' at journalism—there were a lot of other things I could do. I came back to Frank with a long list of job titles. I'm an overachiever, so I felt compelled to name every career I could think of. He helped me narrow down the list to something more manageable. Some were obviously never going to be my thing. Technical writing was a big no—boring. Grant writing—I liked the idea of helping nonprofits, but it didn't seem creative enough. Instructional manuals? Just shoot me!"

They both laughed.

"From the list that remained, we settled on the three careers that seemed the most viable for me. Then, a few weeks later, Frank gave me the names of people who were pretty successful in each of those three areas. He suggested I meet with them to get their perspective on the field and learn about the skills and attributes that were required to be successful. It was a really good idea. It made it more real for me—I could see that there was an actual world of possibility I could tap into.

"Before I met with them," she explained, "Frank and I brainstormed some good questions that I could ask. That helped me a lot. I was nervous about contacting really high-powered people who were all very successful. Why would they want to meet with me? As it turned out, when I mentioned Frank's name, they were very accommodating. And I had more confidence going in because I knew I had some intelligent questions to ask. The meetings were interesting, and I learned a lot.

"After I met with all three of them, I got back to Frank. The first thing he said was, 'Well, Ace? What did you learn?' He had a way of probing and pushing back on my thinking that made me examine many of my biases and assumptions. His questions helped me learn some things about myself—what drove me, and what I really needed in my work to give me the energy and passion to be successful."

"You obviously liked the career path you found," said Rafa.

"Yes, I did. I could see a fit for me. It certainly wasn't boring. As I mentioned in my email, it gave me an opportunity to be part of the action and make an impact right away. And the woman I interviewed who was in marketing actually helped me land a position."

"Rumor has it that you made a big impact in this organization in a very short time." Rafa was looking at her intently.

Cynthia ignored the comment. *Is he brown-nosing me?*

She responded, "My guess is that you are looking to do the same here. And I like that. You aren't afraid to work for what you want. So many of our recent hires want to be instant CEOs, but they don't want to put in the hard work. Clearly, from what you described, you aren't afraid of that—"

"Not at all," Rafa interrupted. "I always try to contribute to the team's success in a really big way. I didn't train that hard just to sit on the bench and watch the other guys perform." He stopped, and his brow furrowed. "I am trying to do that in my current position, but it's a lot harder. I feel like a lot of things are holding me back." He broke eye contact, gazing at the wall behind her head for a moment.

Cynthia noted the change in his mood. The passion that had been in his voice moments before was gone. "We can talk more about what you feel is holding you back, but right now I am going to suggest that we put your work issues on hold for a moment. I want to really get to know you before we drill down to specifics, okay? Once we start dealing with work issues, we may never find our way back."

Rafa refocused. "Sure. What is it you want to know, exactly?"

"I'm curious about the people who influenced your life the most. Tell me a little about them—what they did that made a difference for you."

Rafa thought for a minute. "My influencers? Well, of course I would have to say both my dad and my grandfather. My Nonno— that's my grandfather—especially meant a lot to me. He took me to my first baseball game. And no matter what, he was always patient and willing to listen. I'm named after him, actually—his name is Rafaello and I was called Rafa, just so we wouldn't both answer at the same time. No matter how down or disappointed I was after we lost a game or whatever, he was always there to listen as I rehashed each and every play over and over. He didn't try to talk me out of my feelings. He didn't even try to fix things or tell me what to do. Like, he had special way of just listening."

"Sounds like a very wise grandfather. Is he still alive?"

"He is alive and still kicking! He's ninety-two. I think he will live forever. He says the secret to a long life is a half a glass of red wine every night. For medicinal purposes." Rafa was genuinely smiling now.

"It sounds like a very healthy thing to do," Cynthia said with a smile. "I've been known to take the same medicine!" She was glad the mood had lightened up a bit.

Rafa couldn't stop talking now. "So, other influencers? My idol is Cal Ripken, Jr. Not a Red Sox, but the best. The greatest shortstop in history. His work ethic was a big influence. He always showed up, performed to the max, and never missed a game even when he was hurt. He's always been my role model.

"I also had a coach when I was in high school who meant a lot to me. He wasn't just about playing ball or running drills. He was concerned about how I was doing in my classes and how I was adjusting to prep school. I think he went out of his way to make sure I fit in, since I was a kid out of my element. He was hard on me, but I always felt it was so I would be successful. He pushed me, but for my own good. You know?"

Cynthia nodded, and Rafa paused for a moment. "So, he was my coach. But is that what a mentor does?"

"Good question. People often confuse coaching and mentoring—not surprising, because they are similar in some ways. But they're not the same. I believe that a mentor does what your coach did, and more."

Rafa looked puzzled.

"For example, when I first started presenting to clients, well, let's just say I wasn't as smooth as I appear to be today. My company hired a coach to help me improve my presentation skills. He gave me tips and strategies for delivering material and taught me how to get over my nervousness and how to handle annoying questions and objections. The coaching was very helpful—like the help you got from your baseball coaches. They helped you get into shape, made sure you were using the right techniques. When you weren't hitting well, maybe they took you aside and worked with you?"

"Exactly."

"I call that coaching," said Cynthia. "I think all good mentors are good coaches too. They do give you tips for boosting performance. And they help you with some of your day-to-day challenges. But mostly, as mentors, they are more focused on the future and on your development."

Rafa still looked a bit confused.

"A mentor helps you move along on your career path and prepare yourself to achieve your goals," she continued. "And generally speaking, like me, your mentor isn't your boss and you aren't their direct report. I don't have anything to do with your performance review or your paycheck. If I did, you might not feel as free to be as candid, open, and honest as I hope you will be."

Rafa thought for a moment. This distinction was new for him. "I'm still not sure I get what the difference is," he said. "I get the boss versus coach thing, and I get the boss versus mentor, but I'm not sure I get the coach versus mentor."

Cynthia tried a different approach. "I guess I'm trying to say that coaching is more instructive, but mentoring is more of a relationship. It's not about me telling you what to do and you doing it. We both have some responsibility and learning to do in this partnership. Remember what I told you about Frank Tibbitz? He was there for me when I was down and out. A door had closed, and I didn't know what lay ahead for me. Like your grandfather, he listened and provided support when I was hit with disappointment. But like your dad, he also refused to let me feel sorry for myself. He pointed out my strengths and helped me see where they could best be applied."

Cynthia paused. Rafa was leaning forward now, listening intently.

"That was a very valuable learning experience for me," she continued. "He made sure that I owned my own future and found my own way. He didn't tell me what career to choose, but he helped start me on the search and guided me to some useful resources. Frank used to give me assignments—readings, interviews, to meet with this or that person, and talk to that person, and then come back and tell him what I had learned. All these learning opportunities turned out to be designed for me to discover for myself what it was that I wanted to do. He didn't tell me to move into marketing, but he set up scenarios where I could see it clearly for myself. And he asked me a lot of questions to help me sort out my path. That's what I want to do for you."

She paused. Rafa was quiet, waiting for more.

"I'm not going to hand you a career or a path or a five-year plan," she said. "I am going to be here to help you identify goals that will help you move forward. What do you think?"

Rafa didn't know what to say. This was a lot to take in at once. "Sounds good," he murmured.

Cynthia noted the lull in the conversation and decided it was time to move on. "So, since we are talking about career, you mentioned in your email that one of the things that attracted you to this company was the NextGen Leadership Program. You just finished the year. Tell me about it. What did you like about that experience?"

"It was a good year. Really worth the time and commitment. It gave me more confidence that I know what I'm doing and I'm heading down the right path."

"Sounds like a good start," said Cynthia. "Anything else?"

"Well," said Rafa more slowly, "not having any formal training, it leaves you a bit uncertain about where you stand. They gave us some really practical models and tools. I personally like using a simple model to rely on. Simple models stick with me. I'm not much for a complex theory that leaves me having to figure out how to apply it in the real world. NextGen was all about real stuff. We did case studies that came from the workplace, and we also brought some of our own challenges in to discuss.

I appreciated that. Plus, I met some really cool folks who are now some of the people I go to when I get frustrated or stuck. That's a nice resource. We also got a couple of helpful assessments to give you a neutral, objective look at how you function in your element, why you gravitate to certain kinds of decisions or approaches—like that. It's all helpful."

"I know that they ask NextGen participants to envision what five years down the pike will look like for you—what you want to be doing by then and all that. What was your response to that exercise?"

Rafa sat up taller, and his voice suddenly grew bolder. "I said that I wanted to be leading a new division at CTBN called Strategic Planning Consulting."

"Really? A new division? Interesting idea. What does the Division of Strategic Planning Consulting do?"

Carried away by his own excitement, Rafa described his vision. "We study trends, both externally and internally. We monitor business issues globally and domestically. We are responsible for collecting data from all the divisions and identifying success factors from divisions that are making the grade and figuring out what they are doing versus those groups who aren't making budget. We identify what's holding them back. We report directly to the CEO, and make recommendations about product development, budget allocations, growth, and direction based on our analysis."

He stopped suddenly and smiled. "I know, it's a little like marketing."

Cynthia chuckled. "It is a lot like marketing. We crunch the numbers and monitor trends as well. How might you be different?"

"Our focus is internal financial support. We deploy analysts to each of the five business units and help them prepare for the next eight quarters, in terms of both productivity and budget. We give them real forecasts they can use to plan, but we also function as consultants. We identify red flags, potential threats, and offer alternative scenarios for future planning. We become part of their business team and work collaboratively with them."

Cynthia was impressed. This guy was in the zone. "Rafa, I think that's a great idea. I am sure each of the divisions could use that kind of help. Where did you come up with a concept like that?"

Rafa beamed, pulling his chair a bit closer to the table. "I guess I'm always trying to find ways to be more involved in the success of our internal clients. I can see how they struggle to pull together a budget and set goals for the year. Essentially, they're guessing what their needs will be and what the impact of the economic cycles will be on production and staffing. We have numbers that can help them, but the numbers without the interpretation aren't really of much benefit."

Cynthia wanted to make sure she understood where all this was heading. "So let me see if I understand: it's a way to help the departments by providing more concrete, understandable numbers and showing them how they might apply that information to achieve better results?"

Rafa was relieved. "That's it! You get it! I wish everyone else did."

"You report to Wally Druzey, right? I gather you've shared this idea with your boss and it didn't go over so well with him?

"Good guess. That's exactly what happened."

Cynthia couldn't miss the edge in his voice. Something was definitely going on there. She paused to decide how she wanted to respond. "I am thinking that at some point we will need to talk about what's going on in your current position, but let's make sure we handle it in the right way at the right time. I don't want our mentoring meetings to turn into gripe sessions about your boss. So maybe a bit later we can look at that."

Rafa nodded, serious. "OK, but is the idea that we are going to work on this together and try to make it happen? Like what Frank did for you?"

"Well, there are no magic bullets for success. As Frank told me many times—maybe too many times," she added with a smile—'the rules for success don't work unless you do the work.' And, Rafa, we have work to do together.

"Right now, I have no idea what your future will be and where it will take you. Or what kind of leadership areas you need to develop in yourself in order to move forward. I also want us to focus on what we can accomplish in the year we have together. Your idea about reorganizing our business units isn't something that is going to happen overnight."

Cynthia waited for Rafa to respond. He was silent, clearly thinking about what she had said.

"Yeah," he acknowledged. "There is something to be said for that. I work in a department that likes to take its time before it does anything important. Trust me, it's not about me wanting to make this happen overnight. It's more about, will it happen in my lifetime?"

"Rafa, as your mentor, I want to be an ear for you. I want to listen to your ideas. I want to help you sort through your options. And even though I can see you're a self-starter, sometimes I may need to push you or give you a kick in the pants—metaphorically, of course."

Rafa chuckled. "Actually, I probably could use a kick in the pants from time to time. It sounds like this is going to be just what I need, especially if it will help me get where I want to go."

"So, talking about needs, Rafa, let's talk more specifically about what you want from this relationship and our work together. How do you think I can best help you?"

"Well, I guess for one thing, I would like to have a place to come to. You know, a go-to person to come to who has some answers. I have questions and no one to take them to. So that is number one. And I guess, honestly, I am hoping that this will lead to a promotion. Or at least some way you can help me deal with my boss. And if all else fails, please help me get transferred to a department where I can have more success. Does that work?"

Cynthia leaned back in her chair, consciously slowing down her response time. "Well, yes and no. And also maybe. Here's what I can do." She picked up a pencil and started tapping it on her notepad, emphasizing her points. "I can listen to your questions—and help you sort them out and find answers. I might not give you an answer, but I can help you get there. I can also help you articulate your direction. And I can help you focus so you can leverage your strengths. We can work together to figure out what you need to add to your toolkit to be successful. Like I said earlier, I can give you pushback when I think you need to reconsider your thinking, and I can support your thinking when I feel it is on track. I can do all that."

"Okay, good," said Rafa.

But Cynthia wasn't done yet. She held his gaze and folded her hands together on the table. "Here's what I can't do. I can't get you promoted. That's not what mentoring is about. But I can help you become more promotable."

She stopped for a moment to see Rafa's reaction before she continued. He was still listening, just taking it all in.

"And I can help you identify what has held you back thus far. Like when your coach helped you see why you couldn't hit the curve ball. What do you think, Rafa?"

Rafa gave her a thumbs-up and a rueful smile. "I get it. I get it. It's not what I thought coming in, and I guess maybe I'm a little disappointed, but it is what it is. I can adjust. This is all new for me."

"We're not going to abandon your issues with your boss," Cynthia reassured him. "I can definitely help you with strategies. But I won't end run him, and I won't intercede for you. That's not my job. My job is to push you out of your comfort zone. I don't think you will make the progress you want if you stay comfortable this year. Are you prepared for that?"

Rafa sat back. What he was hearing was not what he had expected, and he knew he needed time to process it. He really wanted this to work, but there was suddenly so much to think about. He hoped he had really picked the right person to mentor him. This was going to be a leap of faith.

Cynthia continued, "So for this to work for both of us—for me as well as for you—I have some expectations of you."

Rafa inhaled deeply and settled deeper in his chair. "Okay, shoot."

"When we get together," said Cynthia, "it won't be business as usual. I don't want this to be all small talk and chitchat. We don't have a lot of time, and I want us to use the time we do have wisely and well. I want us to engage in some high-level and sometimes deep conversations with each other. I will be asking some questions to help you clarify and expand your thinking. And I want us to talk with each other openly, frankly, and honestly. Rafa, I hope you will be real with me. I will be real with you. That is my expectation."

She stopped, made direct eye contact with him, and waited for his response.

But he had already relaxed a fraction, nodding. "I'm OK with that," he said. "That's what we did on our team. No sugar-coating. You got told things straight up, no BSing."

"Well, I'm no baseball coach," Cynthia laughed. "I'm not likely to be that blunt. But I might tell you when I think you're off base. I am pretty sure you can take that."

Rafa reassured her: "I can. I can. I sure hope I can. If I'm not responding in a way you think is appropriate, I hope you'll tell me so. I mean that. I don't want to disappoint you and not know that I'm doing it."

"That's fair and a good point. I will tell you when I think you are not meeting my expectations. Not trying hard enough. Not pushing against your comfort level. Straight-shooting. And I expect you to tell me if something I say is pushing your buttons."

"Phew! I never knew mentoring was going to be so hard." Rafa was already typing some notes into his tablet.

"Hard and, hopefully, productive. One more thing. I think it's important that we talk about our individual learning and communication styles. I remember a conversation I had with Frank when he was giving me feedback about something I had done—he was pretty blunt and direct with me, and I was really upset. I took it as a personal attack, but it was just his way. He hadn't really insulted me, he just hadn't sugar-coated his comments, and I wasn't ready for that. It made me stop listening to him for a while, and he was puzzled. I didn't tell him why I was upset—he had to ask me what was wrong. We got back on track, but it was an eye-opener for me. And for him.

"In a mentoring relationship," Cynthia explained, "this kind of basic misunderstanding is just a time waster. I know now that if we had had a conversation up front about our styles before that happened, it would have helped me understand where he was coming from. I've done considerable reading and learning since then about the concept. Considering that we are going to be focused on learning together, I think we should talk about it together."

"OK," said Rafa, still taking notes, "so you're saying that if you understand my style and I understand yours, it will make things go smoother?"

"Yes, everything: how we build relationships, solve problems, interact with one another, make decisions, and so much more. I'll show you want I mean. Think about a specific time you made a decision or solved a problem." She waited a moment for him to gather his thoughts. "How did you go about it? What process did you use?"

Rafa frowned, thinking. "I don't like process. I make quick decisions. In baseball, you don't have time to think or process. You have to go on instinct. That's what the training is about. In fact, I probably swing too quickly. That's what my coach said. He said that I'm too impatient. And I probably am. Even though I study the numbers, I still go on instinct. Like when I'm at the plate, I don't wait to assess what's coming—how he pitched, what he's got. You know, trends. I just go out there and swing. Sometimes I'd connect, but sometimes I'd strike out. Hit and miss . . . Huh, I never really thought about that before. At work, my impatience gets me in trouble sometimes."

"How, exactly?"

"I sometimes jump in too soon with an answer. I don't like a lot of discussion. Another one of my mantras is 'Just do it!' My style is to listen a bit and make a decision and move on."

"I can relate to that," said Cynthia. "I like results. Talking about a problem for hours drives me up the wall! But I do appreciate taking some time at the beginning of things to make sure everyone on the team understands the ground rules, knows where we're all headed, and has some agreement about how to get there."

Rafa laughed. "Well, I guess that's where we differ. I'm definitely a results person, and I like to tackle problems head on. See it, solve it, move on. I appreciate the value of a team and working together, everybody doing their thing; but to be honest, a lot of teamwork just takes too much time. When everyone has to be happy with a decision, it can become a time waster. So once I have figured it out, got the answer in my head, I don't want to drag the process on and on."

"How do you think our style differences may play out for us in our mentoring relationship?"

Rafa hesitated before he spoke again. "Well, if we end up with an emphasis on sitting together and just talking—you know, about concepts and theory—that's going to drive me crazy. Maybe we could have more of a focus on getting to some action? Like today. We've done a lot of talking and stuff. I mean, I'm excited about all this, but I am chomping at the bit to get started doing something. Show me the action. Let's get to work!"

"I hear what you're saying, Rafa. And believe me, we will get things done together. But we have to find a good balance. I don't want us to pass up some good thinking before we drill down or start implementing something. The first thing that comes to mind might not be the best solution in the long run. And we both may have to work on our patience."

"I will if you will," Rafa said, teasing.

"Like you, I am not afraid to tackle a problem. And I also like to make sure we do something, not just talk about it. Where we may be different is that I tend to focus on the future. Your base-ball training may have emphasized staying in the moment—which makes sense when you're dealing with a ball going ninety miles an hour."

She paused, and Rafa nodded.

"I can certainly relate to the importance of getting things done," Cynthia continued. "Making decisions and moving on. But I am always searching beyond the first good idea for whatever opportunities or possibilities might be out there, ones we haven't thought of yet. You may hear me asking you questions and chal-lenging your current thinking, which might make you uncomfort-able or impatient with me. It comes from me wanting to push you to think beyond the first option in front of you."

"Okay," said Rafa, not looking up from his notes.

"So our styles complement each other in that we like to cut to the chase. But my skin might not be as thick as yours when it comes to taking criticism. Early on, when Frank would push back on my comments, I took it personally. I thought he was being antagonistic. Later I saw that he was actually just being real."

Rafa laughed. "I might be more like Frank in that instance. And I am pretty sure I won't be pushing back at you."

"Never say never." Cynthia smiled.

There was a knock at the door, and Cynthia's assistant stuck his head in to remind her about her next meeting. "Wow, the time has flown, Rafa. It's been a pleasure getting to know you, but we're going to have to wrap this up." She started packing her tote bag. "Before I leave, though, let's talk about what's next for us. And by the way, how do you feel about meeting outside the office? The Bean Counter's Café is just a block away, easy access to the office. Would that work for you? And why don't we meet in two weeks—same day, same time?"

As they both looked at their calendars, Cynthia said, "Let's be sure to build in some time at the next meeting to organize ourselves, lay out a plan, a timetable for what we want to accomplish."

Rafa jumped in: "Can you give me some idea about what's going to happen next? Like, what should I expect in terms of our next meeting? Should I be doing something to prepare?"

"A good question. Why don't you think about your own leadership, what you are looking for, and what ideas you have about what will help you get there. How does that sound?"

"I can do that," Rafa said.

"Good. I have really enjoyed this meeting. I'm looking forward to working with you this year." Cynthia extended her hand.

"Me too," said Rafa, enjoying the firm handshake. "I really appreciate the time. I already feel a little more optimistic about my career from this one meeting. Thank you. I'll see you in two weeks."

———

As Cynthia rode the empty elevator down to the ninth floor for her meeting, she reflected on her hour with Rafa. He was bright and eager and could clearly benefit from the support and guidance of a mentor. But she was certain the relationship was going to require even more work than she had first thought. She didn't want to burst his bubble on his big ideas, but he was going to need some reining in. But how was she going to do that?

He's so single-minded about his organizational goals. I'm going to need to get him to shift focus, to look at developing his own capacity to lead. Cynthia knew it was too early in their relationship to criticize Rafa's plan or be negative, and she was aware that she had stopped herself from pushing back at him several times during their meeting. There were so many things she wanted to say to him . . . *I've got to be patient with myself and with him.*

———

Rafa left the meeting somewhat relieved. He felt that they had connected, and Cynthia liked him, but you never knew. He had been afraid she would be really tough, but she was friendly and open and so smart. Much of what she had told him about mentoring was new to him.

I hope I can do this . . . and get it right, he said to himself. He was a little uneasy about the work part, and it seemed much more structured and formal than he had expected. *I need to make sure she believes in me and my goals.* "Siri," he said to his phone, "remind me to email Cynthia a thank-you note." He stopped and then added, "Siri, remind me to identify some leadership issues to bring to our next meeting."

There, that was done. A good start!

Digging Deeper

Questions for Mentors:

1. Cynthia prepared questions in advance of her first meeting with Rafa. What questions would you prepare prior to your first mentoring meeting?

2. Cynthia spelled out specific expectations she had about Rafa as a mentee. What is the value of articulating expectations early in the relationship?

3. In what ways are your expectations the same as or different from Cynthia's?

4. Cynthia held her first meeting with Rafa in her office. What were the advantages or disadvantages of holding it there? Where would you likely hold the first meeting? Other meetings?

5. Cynthia shared a number of examples of her own vulnerability and inexperience. Did that undermine her credibility with Rafa? How might it have helped their relationship?

6. Cynthia described how she viewed her role as a mentor. Do you agree with her description? What else would you add?

7. What did Cynthia do to build trust in the relationship?

Questions for Mentees:

1. What questions do you have about mentoring?

2. Cynthia spelled out specific expectations she had for her mentee. What is your reaction to her expectations?

3. What expectations do you have about mentoring? Are they the same as or different from Cynthia's?

4. Cynthia held the first mentoring meeting in her office. Would you be comfortable meeting in your mentor's office? Where else might you meet?

5. Cynthia shared a number of stories about her life that revealed her vulnerability and inexperience. Do you think that undermined her credibility? How might it have helped their relationship?

6. Cynthia described how she viewed her role as a mentor. Does her explanation jibe with your perception of the role of a mentor? If not, how is it different?

The Second Meeting:
Taking Care of Business

Cynthia's impatience increased with each passing minute. She'd arrived at the café early to commandeer a private table in the corner, but Rafa was officially late. She hoped that lack of punctuality was not going to be his M.O. She took another sip of her coffee, checked her watch again, and looked up just as Rafa rushed through the doorway.

He sat down and offered a quick apology. "I am so sorry I'm late. Traffic was a mess—"

"You probably need to allow more time," said Cynthia with a sharper tone than she had intended. "Especially now, with all the snowbirds arriving."

"It won't happen again, I promise." He took off his coat, glad to be inside where it was warm. The weather was unusually cold for January, especially this early. He looked longingly toward the coffee line. "No worries, I'll skip the coffee today."

"No, please," said Cynthia, "get your caffeine. I know I wouldn't want to have to start my day without it. I'll wait."

Fortunately, there were only three people ahead of him. Rafa quickly returned to the table with coffee and an energy bar.

As soon as he sat down, Cynthia asked about his week and what had been going on.

Rafa took a quick sip of coffee. "Another week, piece of cake. A no-brainer. I could be doing more. I wish I were doing more. I would like to be challenged more. Nice weekend, though. Got a chance to do a little snowboarding in the mountains with some friends."

"Nice. You can do that with your injury?"

Rafa smiled, thinking about all the fun he'd had. "Yeah, no problem with the leg when I don't have to push off against it.

Snowboarding is easy. Of course, not when you take a header into the snow." He laughed, thinking of one of his recent falls, right in front of a group of young women.

Cynthia laughed with him, relaxing. The image of big, athletic Rafa tumbling head first into a mound of powder amused her. She was glad he could laugh at himself. "So, it's been two weeks since our first meeting. I was wondering what your takeaway was from that session. What were you thinking when you left my office?"

That was a quick topic switch. Rafa paused, clearly unprepared. "Um, let me think a minute," he said, sipping his coffee and hoping it would jog his thinking.

———————

After a minute Rafa said, "You know, after our meeting last week, I was actually relieved."

"Relieved? That's curious. Relieved about what?"

"Going in, I guess I was afraid that you would be like . . . well, like the Iron Lady—you know, the Margaret Thatcher type, all serious, cold, intimidating . . . Not that you look anything like her . . ." Rafa was turning red. "I was relieved that you were so personable and friendly.

Cynthia laughed again. *How old does he think I am?* "And what else? What did you think about the mentoring conversation, for example?"

"Well, that was a bit of a surprise. I think I came in with a different understanding and a different expectation. I didn't know this mentoring thing was going to be so formal and structured."

"Tell me more about that. What did you see as formal and structured?"

"Well, you talked about what our meetings would be like—no small talk and chitchat. I figured that mentoring was about getting to know each other. I thought maybe we'd check in about the week, kind of like what we just did. And you'd be my go-to person if I had issues or concerns. And sometimes we would just talk. Easy and casual. No structure."

Cynthia nodded. "Some of what you're describing is the role of a supervisor, or of a friend, but it's not the role of a mentor. That might be useful and fun for a while. But at some point, if we just focus on what's happening with you day to day, you won't have anything more to talk about and I won't have anything else to add. And I'm not sure you would be much further along in your career development. That's why some structure is needed and process is so important."

Rafa nodded. "Yeah, I started to realize that after a while. After I got home and thought about it, I began to see that you were dead serious about this mentoring thing producing some real results—especially when you said that you wanted me to be real with you and you weren't going to sugarcoat anything. Small talk certainly wouldn't help me with any of the work frustrations I'm feeling. And I do want to move my career forward, which means I need some kind of plan."

"That's right. So that's why we need to put some structure in place, because we need to reach a certain result. We need to achieve a goal within a limited time period. Without some guidelines we can both agree on, I don't think we will get there."

Rafa rubbed his chin and narrowed his eyes.

Cynthia smiled. "Just remember, even though we're in a formal mentoring relationship, our interaction doesn't have to be stilted. It's not that kind of formal."

"Good to hear!" Rafa laughed and took a bite of his energy bar.

"You know, Rafa, I've had had several people in the course of my career who were my informal mentors. I called them when I needed an answer or a point of view. If I wasn't sure what direction to take, or wanted to bounce an idea off of them, I'd pop into their office. It was on my terms, and what I did with the information was up to me. Have you ever had anyone in your career or someone in your life that you used like that?" Cynthia waited, letting him consider the question.

"Sure," Rafa said. "Certainly when I was struggling at bat, I had some people I would call to get some help."

"So in those situations, you could take away what you wanted from the time together. Use it or not."

"Yeah."

"But there was no real accountability. It was very casual, and very easy. No agreements or regularity. Right? So sometimes with Frank, for example, I would follow up and tell him what I did as a result of his input, and sometimes not."

She paused to make sure Rafa was following, then continued: "I see our formal mentoring commitment as different. We will agree on how we'll work together, set a timeframe, and work together on goals that you identify to help you move your career forward. And we will be putting in place a game plan to get there."

"Ah," said Rafa, "now you're talking my language. At BC our coach made every player sign a personal letter of commitment about how we would conduct ourselves, approach our training, all of that."

Cynthia was pleased to hear that he approved and even had some experience with the idea of plans and agreements and follow through. That hadn't been the case with some of her other mentees.

"That was a good idea your coach had," she said. "It made you understand that being on the baseball team was a commitment. There was a give, something you had to contribute, and a get, a benefit you received. There were expectations. So we also should craft some agreements. Ours should be more about how we will work together so we can stay on track and be successful. I am investing my time and energy in this, and I want to see a return on my investment. That's my give and my get.

"Did your coach spell out some of the expectations he had for players to be on the team? I am sure he did. I think some guidelines for how we work together will get us there."

Rafa's brow furrowed. "What do you mean by guidelines? Like what, for example?"

"Well, at the most basic, how often do you want to meet? Given what we are going to try and accomplish, how much time do you need from me?"

Cynthia paused to allow Rafa time to consider the questions and make some suggestions.

"Is there a general rule of thumb?" he asked. "I don't want to be a burden, hounding you all the time, but I also want to have enough time to accomplish something. I've never done this before. I don't really know what to expect or what is reasonable. What do you think works best?"

"Well, I think in the beginning, as we try and get a focus on things, maybe once every two weeks might work. How does that sound?"

Rafa was relieved to hear that she was going to make herself that available. It reinforced in his mind that she was really committed to his success. "Sounds great."

"Good, so maybe an hour, every two weeks. But that doesn't mean we can't have contact outside that. If you need to touch base in between with a question or an issue, just drop me an email. I don't want to leave you hanging with a problem for two weeks until we meet."

"I'd appreciate that—I know your time is valuable."

"Maybe we won't need to meet as frequently later on, but let's make sure you get a good running start. Does this location and time work for you? Or do you want to try something else?"

"This is fine; I can be here. I'll get an earlier start next time."

"Well, it's good for me; it gets me going early, and I can still get to work on time. Let's plan on an hour every other week and assess if it's still working for us in a couple of months. Are we good?"

"Good to go! But what happens if one of us is traveling or can't make it? You must be on the road a lot."

"That can and will happen, Rafa. I am willing to take responsibility if I have to change our plans. Why don't we make a deal that the person who cancels a meeting be responsible for rescheduling, OK?"

"OK."

"I do have a grinding schedule," Cynthia acknowledged. "I normally don't like to overplan, but I am going to suggest we get our dates on the calendar up front, at least for the first ninety days. We can change as we go, but at least we'll have some dates and times we can count on."

"Great. So we are going to nail down dates and meet every other week for an hour before work. Wally—you know, my boss— will like that because it won't be taking up any of my time on the job. I am not sure he's a big fan of this arrangement."

"Oh, I'm glad you mentioned that. Sometimes supervisors aren't exactly sure about what goes on inside a mentoring relationship. I've known a few supervisors in my day who got paranoid when their direct reports were being mentored by senior management. I suspect they were a bit afraid they were part of the conversation and it was going to reflect poorly on them. It can make a supervisor or manager uncomfortable."

"Is there a way to avoid that? I don't want Wally to become any more annoyed with me than he already is."

This is the second time he's mentioned Wally in two minutes. "I'm glad you brought that up. What do you think might help keep him from being worried about our meeting arrangement?" She gave Rafa a moment to consider.

"How about this idea?" said Rafa. "I can give him a summary of what we talk about. That would keep him in the loop."

"Well, it certainly might help him feel better, but I think it might create another kind of problem. A while back, when I was internal communications manager in another organization, I had a direct report who was struggling with one of our managers. He couldn't get reliable numbers from him in a timely way, and he came to me for help. I said that my experience with this guy was that he was unreliable in other areas as well, and that you had to ride herd on him to get anything done.

"Well, a week later, this manager came marching into my office and told me that he'd heard that I had a problem with his follow-through. That was an awkward moment! I had just assumed that my direct report knew I'd shared my opinions with him in confidence and that he had the good judgment not to repeat it. I was wrong. That manager was very angry and appropriately so. Our relationship was never really comfortable after that."

"No kidding!" said Rafa.

"So, now that we've agreed on where and when we're meeting, we obviously need to talk about the confidentiality between us. I don't want to make any assumptions about how you interpret my intention, and vice versa." She looked Rafa in the eye and waited.

"I'm glad we're talking about this," said Rafa. "I certainly don't want what I say to you to go any further. I have a career; I've got to protect it. What happens in Vegas stays in Vegas, right?"

"Right." Cynthia smiled. It wasn't the first time she'd heard that one from a mentee. "So I think we are both saying it's important that we keep what we say to ourselves. I am going to assume what you tell me is in confidence. I want you to do the same. That baseline of trust is important to me. Otherwise, I have to start editing what I say to you, and I don't want to do that. And I don't want to think you're holding back because you're afraid what you say is going to get around the whole organization."

Rafa leaned forward and lowered his voice for emphasis. "Totally agreed. I was freaking out a little last night about who was going to hear feedback about our conversations, my progress, or what you thought of me after our last meeting. I wasn't sure if this mentoring thing is really part of a performance review, or an assessment of my potential for leadership, and you'd be reporting back to the leadership team so that they know if I have what it takes. That kind of stuff."

"Thank you for being so forthright. It takes a lot of courage to put that on the table, and those are all good things to clarify. I want to assure you that our mentoring relationship is not part of a promotion assessment, a performance review, or a vehicle for feedback to management about your potential. Because if what you said to me was going to have a direct impact on your future, your salary or getting a new position, you might be more cautious about what you say. You might say something you think I want to hear rather than what you are really thinking."

"I probably would," he said, almost to himself. "Yeah, I probably would. I guess I definitely would!" He laughed. "Glad I don't have to worry about that one."

Cynthia paused and then summarized their agreement. "So we agree that what we say here stays here, between us. And if I run into Wally and he asks me what we're talking about, or how you're doing, I am going to say that I am enjoying the interaction, and I am not going to provide any specifics. I agree not to share the substance of our discussions—that is, unless you give me express permission. And vice versa. It works two ways, OK?"

"Absolutely," said Rafa, nodding in agreement.

"Anything else you'd like to add?"

"Yes," he said immediately. "Here's one. I feel kind of silly asking this, but what exactly are these meetings going to cover? Are you going to prepare a topic, or an agenda? I don't start any game without knowing who is in the lineup."

"Another set of really good questions, Rafa. I've seen too many mentoring meetings become what I call 'three cups of coffee.' With each cup of coffee, it is the same old thing: 'How's it going?' 'How's it going?' 'How's it going?' Then the relationship fizzles out because there is nothing substantive to focus conversation on. You know what I mean?"

Rafa nodded, sipping his coffee.

"That's why I am a great believer in agendas," Cynthia continued. "They keep you focused. At the same time, I also don't want our meetings to be too regimented and restrictive. I want to hear what's going on in your world. And I also want to make sure there is time to hear how you are progressing with whatever goals and leadership issues we develop together."

Rafa was clearly puzzled. "So what *do* we talk about?"

"How about if we do what we just did this morning? We start with a little catch-up on the last two weeks. You know, like what's going on for you and me, but we limit the time we spend on it. We might look at anything we've discussed earlier, or something you were working on, and talk about how that is going. For example, if I sent you an article to read, we would be discussing it. If I sent you a question to think about, we would talk about that. And if you sent me a question that you were struggling with or wanted to discuss, then that's what we would be spending some time on."

She looked for confirmation that Rafa understood, then continued. "And then a big chunk of our time, certainly the next couple of meetings, you and I would spend trying to sort through your leadership development goals and nailing down what we want to work on together. My experience is that this is hard to do, and it takes work. It needs time, and it needs to be done well if you are going to have any meaningful results. What do you think about that?"

"It sounds like our meetings might take more than an hour, that's what I think!"

"Well, we can assess that as we go. Maybe build in some flexibility when we can, or when we anticipate needing more time. Meanwhile, before each of our meetings, I would like you to own the responsibility of setting the agenda. Since it should focus on what concerns you, I am going to suggest you drive this."

"Excellent," said Rafa.

"Your agenda doesn't have to be as formal as the one we use for our Ops meetings, but it should outline the key areas and issues you want to discuss during our hour. Put your agenda together a couple of days before we are scheduled to meet, and email it to me at least a day ahead. That way I know what you are thinking about and issues you are working on. It will help ensure that both of us come prepared. If I have anything to add to the agenda, I will send back my suggestions. Are you up for that?"

Rafa gave her a thumbs-up.

"Excellent," Cynthia said.

Cynthia flipped through her notes. "OK, I think we've established a good basis for how we can work most effectively together. We have some time allocated for meeting, and we talked about confidentiality. We know the general focus of our conversations, and we know we will come prepared using the agenda you are setting for us. That should keep us on course." She put a check next to each item she listed, to make sure she didn't miss anything.

"But just to be sure," she said, "let's check in on all of this in March, around the ninety-day mark, to make sure it is all still working for us. From my experience, that's usually a good time to talk about what we could be doing better and if we think we need to make some midcourse corrections."

"Right," said Rafa. "Maybe I just set a reminder in my calendar to make sure to include that on the agenda at the ninety-day mark."

Cynthia waited until he was done. "OK, great. Now, I've got one new topic to add to our agreement."

"Shoot," said Rafa.

"I know you have some issues with your boss that you want to work out," Cynthia began. "I certainly want to help you address them, but let's make it constructive. Like I said before, I don't want our meetings to end up being a gripe session about Wally and what's happening at work. We need to build towards the future and not get stuck on day-to-day issues. Agreed?"

"I got it. No whining. I don't think I am much of a complainer anyway. Or, at least, I hope I'm not," he said with a smile.

Cynthia looked down at her watch. She had a meeting to get to after this. "It looks like we have about twenty minutes left. How do you want to spend the rest of our time today?"

Rafa paused, thinking. He'd been looking at a poster on the wall behind Cynthia's chair. It was quote from someone named Anaïs Nin. He'd never heard of her, but her words really got his attention: "Dreams are necessary to life."

"Well," he began slowly, "maybe we should talk about the leadership development goal some more? I really do have my eye set on creating and running the Strategic Planning Consulting division in five years. That's my goal, plain and simple!"

"Good," said Cynthia. "Let's take a look at that goal in its current form. I've actually been thinking about it since our last meeting."

Rafa smiled, gratified.

"It seems to me that your goal has two components. One is about reorganizing our business unit by creating a new division. While I think that has some merit, it really is beyond the scope of our work to get that goal initiated during this relationship."

Rafa's face fell, but Cynthia forged ahead. She wanted to give him a reality check, not shut him down.

"I'm pretty sure we would be butting our heads against a wall for a year to try and get the attention and support of key leaders on that one," she explained. "And I'm not sure what progress we would have made by the end of it. If our focus is solely on reorganization, we wouldn't be paying any attention to you and your development. But the other component is more accessible: eventually, you want to become a division leader. Given where you are right now, do you think you are ready for the next step?"

Rafa had been periodically taking notes as Cynthia was speaking. He looked up and met her eyes, taking a deep breath. "Well, what I think and what Wally thinks are probably two different things, but I guess I would have to honestly say no. I am not ready . . . not ready yet."

"Then maybe we should start to work in that arena. What goal do you think would be a good focus for us?"

Rafa stared at the table for a moment before he looked back at Cynthia. "Maybe preparing me to become a division leader in a couple of years?" He tilted his head and waited.

Cynthia grinned. "I like it. And I like it because that goal is about you being seen as a leader. That's not about convincing Wally; it requires some real inner work. You are going to need to examine your strengths and challenges. What are you doing that's working for you, and what's working against you? We'll need to talk about the new skills, knowledge, and talents you will need to acquire, and how to leverage your current assets. And we'll need to explore what's holding you back from getting to the next level."

Cynthia paused to sip her coffee and let Rafa catch up with his notes; then she continued. "All of that 'work' will lead to the next step. And that, in turn, will help you prepare yourself for the position you want. Now do you see why I said, 'No sugar-coating'?"

Rafa nodded, looking chagrined. *This is way more work than I bargained for. Doesn't she know how many hours I work just to get my own projects done?*

"Are you willing to tackle some of these thorny questions? They can be tough."

"I can handle it." He tapped out the last few points and looked at his watch.

"OK, good. Before we pack up, let's back up and talk about the big picture—we still have a couple of minutes."

Cynthia asked, "Have you ever read Stephen Covey's book *7 Habits of Highly Effective People?*"

"I've heard of it, but I haven't read it." He noted the book title in his tablet.

He pays attention, Cynthia observed silently. "One of my favorite quotes is in that book: 'Begin with the end in mind.'"

"'Begin with the end in mind.' I like it." Rafa made a note.

"Well, imagine that it's five years from now and you *are* a division leader. Really try to picture yourself. What are you doing? How are you acting and thinking differently from how you are right now? How would people describe your leadership attributes in the role? What is helping you achieve your success? Is it your knowledge? And if so, what knowledge? What is it you are consistently doing that is demonstrating your success?"

Rafa wrote frantically to capture all the questions and then stopped to read what he'd jotted down. "Whoa—those are a lot of questions. Do you want me to answer them now? Because really I can't come up with anything this quickly."

Oops, information overload. Cynthia pulled back. "You're right, absolutely right. It's too soon to be able to respond to those issues. You need time to reflect on your answers. We need to start somewhere else before we get there. Tell me, Rafa, is there someone that you know and admire who is currently a director at CTBN?"

Uh-oh. Rafa didn't want to accidentally give the wrong answer, name some guy she disliked, and risk not getting her stamp of approval. "Um, how about Alan Weber, the operations director? I think he's pretty good. What do you think of him?"

Cynthia withheld her opinion, purposely ignoring the last part of the question. Instead, she asked him why he thought Alan was a good director and what qualities he admired in him.

"Well, for one thing, he always seems to get results. I've sat in his Ops meetings, and I like that he shares the data with his people, and he compares it to quarterly goals. You always know where you stand with him. That's one thing, one very important thing."

"So he posts the numbers. And we know how you like numbers." She smiled. "So, what else do you admire?"

"He seems to be really good on his feet with strategy. He's a good problem solver. For example, when production comes up short, he's quick with good ideas: how to boost inventory, move stock around, or tweak a timetable. And he's smart. Really, really smart. I guess I admire that." Rafa exhaled. "So, what do you think of him?"

Cynthia replied, "I agree with your assessment of Alan on results and strategic thinking. He is smart and he is quick. He can solve a problem."

Without missing a beat, Rafa chimed in: "I sense a 'but.'" *Damn. I did pick the wrong guy.*

"Well, it's more of an 'and.' And here's one of those confidentiality issues. I expect my comments to remain between us." She shot him a look.

"They will. I keep my word. So what's up with 'and'?"

"And the ideas are always *his*. I'm not sure that he lets his people participate in problem solving, even though they are the ones who have to deal with the problem and they know it best."

"Huh. I really hadn't thought about that. I hate it when bosses do that to me. Are you saying that one of the qualities of a good director is to let your people solve the problems, and not solve them for them?"

"What do you think? Is that attribute important to you?"

"Totally. My director doesn't involve me or anyone from our group in the bigger problems. And yes, it makes us all feel devalued. Why are we even there? Personally, I have plenty to contribute, and I don't often get a chance to make much of a contribution. So I guess I would say yes, emphatically, it's very important to me."

"Rafa, I think one of the hardest things for a leader to do is to resist the temptation to solve problems and make all of the decisions alone. I know it's easier to do it that way. For one thing, no one is fighting you. After all, you aren't going to argue with yourself. And most of us think we have the right answer anyway. It is a lot quicker because you don't have to take time to get other people up to speed. And if it is a good result, by the way, you get the credit. You get to be the hero. Clearly, there is a big payoff to making decisions on your own."

Rafa could feel something shift in his perspective. "Wow," he said, shaking his head. "I never saw it that way."

"This is actually one of the biggest personal challenges in my role. I have bright, sharp people who work for me, and they want to be in on the action. I can tell you, whenever I announce a decision that I've made and handed down to them, I usually get resistance. They push back—hard. And they also push back if I ask for their input or recommendation and then don't consider it seriously or do a 180 on them. Trust me, that's even worse because it seems like I am just trying to appease them without taking them seriously."

"It sounds like you're damned if you do and damned if you don't," said Rafa.

Cynthia spoke in a rush, barely stopping to take a breath: "Decision making is tricky business. When you are a leader you are not just leading a division, a department, or a business unit; you are leading people. That means that you're responsible for facilitating their development. My job is to help my people learn how to think strategically and make critical decisions. The only way you can do that is to provide opportunities for them to participate meaningfully. In fact, sometimes I have to catch myself and ask, 'Should I be deciding this or should I let them make the decision?' Trust me, I get it wrong sometimes, and my team lets me know it.

"It's hard for me, but I'm going to have to exercise self-discipline and resist the temptation to give you answers. I want to hear your ideas and help you find your own solutions. So," she ended with a smile, "mentoring is good practice for me to get better at listening, and it makes me a better leader of my own team."

Rafa was caught off guard by Cynthia's candor. He hadn't expected her to open up about the problems she had faced as a leader. "But if we're talking about leading a division—well, that's a lot of responsibility. You can't risk having your people make a bad decision and then having to clean up the mess yourself."

"You're right, Rafa. That's partly why it's tough. You have to weigh the pros and cons. You have to weigh the timing and convenience—and, of course, the outcomes and risks. It's easy to talk yourself into making the decision because of the risks and outcomes. It's easy to fall back on yourself. Plus, once you decide to involve your team, you have to set them up for success. You have to take the time to bring them up to speed on the issues and give them the background they need. To leverage all that, you need to define the parameters and scope of their authority. If you want them to select the vendor for a new piece of equipment, they have to be aware of the budget. You don't want them choosing a Mercedes when all you have in your budget is a Honda Civic. It's complicated."

"Can you elaborate?" Rafa was listening intently. This was really inside baseball now, what he had hoped for from mentoring.

"Once my team makes a decision and I approve it," Cynthia said, "it's all hands on deck. My team is fully behind it. They completely understand it. They are motivated. They are engaged. They feel like owners. You can't hold them back." Suddenly Cynthia's expression changed and she looked at her watch. She realized that her enthusiasm had gotten the better of her and she had been talking way too much.

"Wait a minute. Sorry. I got caught up and carried away. This isn't supposed to be a leadership seminar. I got us off track. I don't want to do all the talking. I fell into my own trap."

Rafa interjected, "But you were talking about some issues that are important in the director role—"

"Don't worry, we'll deal with that more down the line, I'm sure." She looked at her watch. "I guess that's it for today anyway; we're out of time."

And to make her point, she began to pack up.

Cynthia stopped and looked up. "Rafa, before you close up your tablet, I thought of one more thing—would you be willing to write up all the things we agreed to earlier? I saw you making all those notes."

"Sure, no problem," Rafa said, making another note.

"Good. Can you include our agreements about the time, confidentiality, agenda, et cetera? I know it will be a very helpful reminder for us to have that recorded in a document somewhere. And since you're handling the agenda, how about including your issue? Maybe we could drill down more on understanding what's expected at the director's level.

"And one more quick thought," she added as she put on her coat. "Do you think looking at a current job description for director would be useful? Would that help you?"

"I never even thought about that, but of course, that's a great idea." Rafa made another note.

"Well, it might be a good start anyway. Why don't you talk to the folks at HR before our next meeting and see if you can pick one up? We can review it together and assess how it compares to your own skill sets."

Cynthia stood up, ready to go, as Rafa continued to jot down notes. "OK, Rafa. Got to run now. Please remember to send me an agenda before the next meeting."

"Will do. And thanks, Cynthia. I am juiced. Really. And not just from the caffeine. I really feel excited that I might actually get my career going. At least I'm focusing on something that is related to my career instead of just spinning my wheels. It's energizing."

"I'm glad you feel that way, Rafa. That's why we're here. And I'm glad that we have a focus and a game plan. I'm looking forward to our next meeting in a couple of weeks."

With a sheepish grin, Rafa offered a parting shot: "And don't be late!"

Rafa stopped typing as Cynthia walked away. He let out a deep breath and relaxed into his chair, finishing off what was left of his coffee. *All in all,* he thought, *that went pretty well.* Yes, he'd been late, but she'd let it go quickly. And she'd shared a lot of new information with him—a lot. He had to admit that he had entered into this mentoring arrangement without any real understanding of what it was about except that it would help him in his career. He wondered if maybe he was in over his head.

Coaching was something he understood; he'd worked with coaches on refining his swing and footwork for over a decade. This mentoring arrangement, though, seemed a lot more formal, and it had taken him by surprise. Had it shown on his face? He didn't think so. At first, when Cynthia started talking about putting guidelines and rules in place, he felt like he was back in school. But as he reflected on it, she was probably right. Having an agreement about where, how, and what their mentoring conversations would cover could make him focus and prepare. *So, OK. I can do this.*

Once that clicked into place, Rafa began to feel excited and optimistic about the whole thing. He had a sudden glimpse of the future: with Cynthia's help, he might actually move his career in the right direction, even turbocharge it. *Yes!* He found himself smiling and fist-pumping, and he looked around quickly. The other customers had their eyes on their laptops.

He was surprised that Cynthia was so open. He couldn't believe she'd actually told him about the time that remarks she thought had been confidential blew up in her face, and the time that her team got angry with her for bypassing them in a decision. It definitely made her more human—everyone made mistakes. And he felt respected because she trusted him with her story. But he honestly didn't know if he would be able to reciprocate.

Digging Deeper

Questions for Mentors:

1. Rafa mentioned that he thought mentoring was going to be an "informal drop-in when he needed help, not so formal and structured." What are the benefits of a structured relationship? What are its disadvantages?

2. How might structure help you facilitate your mentee's learning? What structures exist in your current mentoring relationships? Do you need to add more or less structure?

3. Cynthia tells Rafa that mentoring partners can get bogged down in the day-to-day and lose sight of long-term goals. How much time do you spend talking about day-to-day issues versus long-term goals and development? Is it sufficient?

4. Cynthia and Rafa developed some agreements to keep their relationship on track. Which of Cynthia and Rafa's agreements would you want to adopt? What other agreements might you put into place?

5. Confidentiality is critical to a successful relationship, yet many mentoring partners fail to discuss it early in their relationship. How do you understand confidentiality in a mentoring relationship? What can be shared and what can't be shared? Have you adopted a confidentiality agreement with your mentoring partners?

6. Even though Rafa identified one of Cynthia's colleagues as a leader he admired, Cynthia questioned the effectiveness of this colleague's shared decision-making skills. Do you think Cynthia was appropriate in her comments? How would you have handled this situation?

Questions for Mentees:

1. Rafa thought mentoring was going to be an "informal drop-in when he needed help, not so formal and structured." What are the benefits of a structured relationship? What are its disadvantages?

2. What structures exist in your current mentoring relationship?

3. How much time do you spend talking about day-to-day issues with your mentor versus your long-term goals and

development? What happens when you restrict your focus to day-to-day issues? What do you gain? What do you lose?

4. Cynthia and Rafa developed some agreements to keep their relationship on track. Which agreements would you want to adopt? What other agreements might you want to add?

5. Confidentiality is critical to a successful relationship, yet many mentoring partners fail to discuss it early in their relationship. What does confidentiality mean to you? What are your assumptions about confidentiality in a mentoring relationship?

6. Even though Rafa identifies one of Cynthia's colleagues as a leader he admires, Cynthia questions the effectiveness of this colleague's shared decision-making skills. If you were Rafa, would you have been put off or was it OK for her to point out his weakness?

The Third Meeting: Let's Get Real

Rafa walked into the café, scanned the room, and heaved a sigh of relief. *Good.* He was the first to arrive. In fact, he was twenty minutes early. He smiled, hoping that Cynthia would note his punctuality and see that he was taking her feedback to heart. He grabbed a seat at a table and checked his email, glancing up frequently, trying to spot Cynthia as she walked in.

During the last two weeks he'd done everything she'd asked him to do, but it had been much harder than he'd anticipated. He felt uncomfortable opening up and sharing his problems with someone he didn't know all that well and who could potentially give him a thumbs-down on future promotions, no matter what reassurances she offered. He felt uncomfortable opening up to people, period, except Nonno. He really hoped this mentoring wasn't going to turn into some sort of therapy session—that was not why he was here.

His grandfather had been the exception. Even when Rafa didn't acknowledge that something was bothering him, Nonno would sense his upset or uneasiness. He would sit down next to Rafa and put his hand on his knee, tilt his head, and just say, "So . . .?" And Rafa's problems would come pouring out. Rafa could tell him anything. He never felt judged, or afraid that what he said would come back to haunt him—which had not been the case in other parts of his life.

When he gave his life over to competitive sports at age eight, two messages had repeatedly been drilled into his psyche:

- Don't let the other team see you sweat.

- Never reveal your weaknesses or injuries—the other side will take advantage if they know your vulnerabilities.

That philosophy had worked well in his short-lived base-ball career. Now, at work, he carried on with the same mindset. Business was a competition too.

Years of practice had taught him to keep his worries and fears to himself, to look like nothing was bothering him. Concerned that showing doubt made him appear weak and would undermine people's confidence in him, he avoided asking for help or relying on others. For the most part, he had figured things out for himself. And he thought he'd done a fairly decent job.

This mentoring relationship, however, was brand-new ter-ritory. He wondered if he could live up to what Cynthia had in mind. He understood that it would take time, and that her goal was to see him succeed, but he wasn't sure about those real con-versations she had talked about early on. He'd flinched when she said, "I expect you to be real," but he didn't think she'd noticed. He still wasn't quite sure how being real was going to play out.

What he did know was that mentoring was going to require work on his part, not just having meetings and talking to one another—what Cynthia had called "chitchat." And he wasn't going to be able to rely on her to steer the direction of their talks; she wanted him to drive the relationship, although he wasn't sure what that meant beyond setting the agenda. She had approved the agenda he'd emailed her, so that was good, he guessed.

He wished she'd show up so he could stop thinking about all this and just start the meeting.

Cynthia was feeling stressed by project deadlines as she headed toward the coffee shop. She had just returned from the UK, where she had been at a weeklong marketing exposition, and she could feel the jet lag tugging at her brain. It had been a pretty excit-ing conference. She had learned about some new revenue streams her company could develop via social media, and she was eager to explore them. And then there was all the work that had piled up when she was away. She had to admit that meeting with Rafa was not the top item on her list today.

She looked down and noticed her hands gripping the steering wheel. *Come on, girl, this isn't fair to Rafa. Don't take it out on him. You wouldn't have liked it if Frank had ever made you feel like you were in the way.* She pulled into her parking space and centered herself for a moment. *OK, ready to go.* She could use that coffee this morning. She walked the short block to the Bean Counter's Café in record time.

On the way in, she glanced at the clock and realized that she was five minutes early. Rafa waved and caught her eye. She walked toward his table and then noted the half cup of coffee in front of him. She smiled, pleased with his effort to be there on time. "Good to see you here, nice and early."

He raised his cup of coffee. "You only have to tell me once and I get it."

Cynthia excused herself to go order her coffee, but Rafa was eager to get started. "Wait, I'll come with you!" Queued up in line, Rafa referred to the agenda and asked her if that was what she had expected.

"Yes, it looks good."

Rafa smiled. "Do you want me to start?"

"Well, wait. Let's slow it down, Rafa. How are you doing? What's new?"

"It's been a crazy couple of weeks. Busy. I guess the busy is good. You know, I like to be in the thick of things." He went on a bit as Cynthia ordered a skinny vanilla latte. Coffee in hand, they walked back to the table.

"So, Rafa, what did you do that was fun this weekend?" Cynthia settled into her chair, and sipped her coffee slowly.

"Well," he said, "my girlfriend and I went to a concert. Fun." He wasn't sure if it was appropriate to ask the same question but he did, cautiously. "Did you get to do anything fun?"

"I just returned from a weeklong conference in England. This time the jet lag really got me, and I spent the weekend catching up on sleep and work. So I'm slammed right now, really slammed, and . . . a little edgy."

"Too bad. England sounds great. I hope you got some down time when you were there. Do you usually have to work weekends?"

"No, not usually. And I don't like to. But my work is piling up as we speak, so let's gets started."

Rafa grabbed his agenda, cleared his throat, and read out the first item. "So this first part is catching up. I've allocated about ten minutes for it. Then, as you can see, I have fifteen minutes set for reviewing the job description of the director position that I attached—your suggestion from the last meeting. And then thirty minutes on moving the goal forward. And a five-minute wrap-up. Is that too structured for you? Just checking."

Cynthia shook her head. "No, I don't think so. It's broad enough to keep us focused, but not limiting. Let's try it."

"Good," said Rafa. "So, to catch up—I'd really like your opinion on something that happened in our department last week. We are working on this big presentation to the CFO and some department heads. My whole group is providing input and recommendations, but I'm the one responsible for making this presentation."

"That's great," said Cynthia.

"Yeah, but it's also my problem: I'm the one who's up there—I'm the face of the entire group—and I need to be credible. But I feel like the recommendations that I am getting from the team are bogus, they're never going to work. I know that I'm right and they're wrong. I'm really stuck. I'm supposed to go along with the team, but I just can't bring myself to stand up in front of these honchos and know that they're judging me by someone else's bad idea. One day these people may influence my career, and this presentation might be the deal breaker. I am totally frustrated. What do you think?"

"Well, obviously, this is a pretty tough issue to deal with," she replied.

"I guess that's some consolation."

"Some. But it doesn't make it any less difficult. Is the recommendation right or wrong? Or are you right or wrong? What is it you are really asking?"

Rafa was clearly looking to Cynthia to validate and support his position. If she didn't, she realized, it could dampen his enthusiasm. Yet she didn't want to be inauthentic, and she had said early on that she would be direct with him. Now she was going to have to make good on her word. She was going to have to push back against some of his ideas in a way that supported him but that also challenged him to learn and grow. *Be careful*, she admonished herself.

"If I said to you, 'Rafa, you're wrong,' how would that make you feel?"

"I guess I would be upset. Disappointed. I don't like being wrong."

"Well, there you are. And what stance do you take when someone tells you that you're wrong?"

"Dig in, probably. I'm a fighter."

"I can be one too. So if I hold a position that's opposite to yours, and we are both fighters, what do we have?"

"War!" Rafa roared. They laughed in unison.

"See, now you are right. We have a battle. Over what? We don't even remember the issue. We're just fighting for our position and the insistence of not being found to be wrong. Making every issue right or wrong invariably encourages people to fight harder for their idea, even a lame one. And I've learned—on more than one occasion, unfortunately—that with right and wrong, you can win the battle but lose the war."

He was nodding in agreement, so she continued. "Your team predicament may be one of those situations. If you prove you're right, your teammates may never want to work with you again. Right now, you don't want to work with them. So, in the end, do you succeed or fail?"

Rafa stared at the wall for a moment and said, "They just don't have the guts to present something that might be bolder. They play it safe. It's like the top of the eighth and the tying run is on second. There are no outs, and you get the sign to bunt. You've been hitting .338 and you're on a roll. You want the coach to give you the sign to hit away. Bunt? Lame. Go with strength."

Cynthia sighed at yet another baseball analogy. She began to wonder if they sounded as tiresome and hackneyed to other people as they did to her. But she decided to put the baseball issue on hold for now.

"I agree with you on several issues," she began. "First, you should never get in front of anyone and say something you don't believe, or take a position you can't back. Eventually, you will be found out and you'll develop a reputation as a BSer—or, worse yet, someone who is untrustworthy. Then who would believe anything else you said? The first time a leader pushes back on the idea to test your mettle, you will cave."

Rafa was quiet, listening hard.

"I can't tell you how many times I have seen a presenter respond to an objection with, 'Well, it wasn't my idea. I told them it wouldn't work. Don't blame me.' So you might win the battle there. It might be a bad idea and you pointed it out, but guess what those senior leaders will remember? That the presenter was weak. He lacked courage or he lacked principles, and he threw his people under the bus. In any case, you lose the war and you reputation is tarnished."

Rafa was perplexed. "So what do I do? What would you do?"

"Well, first of all, I try not to think in terms of right or wrong. I've learned over time that rarely is something or someone completely right or completely wrong. There are times when an idea or strategy has merit, and sometimes timing makes it less advantageous. In this case," Cynthia said, "I'd split the difference. Are there areas of the proposal where you can incorporate some of your team members' ideas? Not just to placate them, but in earnest—without compromising overall quality?"

Cynthia could see that Rafa was ambivalent. He wanted to be right, but he had gotten the point about not getting involved in battles of right versus wrong.

"You know, Rafa, a consolidated plan might actually improve the idea as a whole, but you have to engage in this kind of mental effort with a constructive attitude. It begins with you. To do this successfully, you have to begin by focusing on positive aspects of your team's ideas instead of what is wrong with their ideas. It takes real discipline to pull this off. So let me ask you: Did you spend enough time looking at their recommendations from the vantage point of what was beneficial and could work?"

Rafa shrugged and took a sip of coffee. "Well, maybe not in quite in that way. Maybe a quick pass at it. And, FYI, it didn't get us anywhere."

———

Cynthia went at it from another angle, trying to get him to stop taking his position personally. "So, how would a leader go about solving this problem? If you—Rafa—were the leader of this team—like the director of the Strategic Planning Division—how would you get this problem turned around? Be objective."

Rafa took a few seconds to think and then launched in. "I would start by calling a team meeting with all the players in the dugout for the sole purpose of looking for ways to strengthen the recommendations. I would probably give a pep talk about a great start. And I'd also suggest there might be ways to take it to the next level."

"Good idea. I would do the same. What next?"

"Well, first I would remind the team about what we were try-ing to improve or accomplish with our recommendations. And then, to your point earlier, I'd ask them to be disciplined and focus on getting them to talk about what they like about the plan. By acknowledging their effort, and pointing out the positive parts of their ideas, I think I could make people who are not on board with me actually want to play ball."

Cynthia liked how he was processing the problem. He'd turned it around quickly. "Nice approach."

Rafa was on a roll, enjoying the exercise. "Then I would lead a discussion about the downside, the potential risks. Capture those. Finally, I would move to innovative thinking, trying to get the team to think outside the box. Ask for big, bold ideas that we might consider. Not examining the risks at this time, just throw them up and consider the ramifications later. See what jells. So, basically, the positives, the negatives, and then the creative options. How does that all sound?"

"I think it sounds great." She paused, and then challenged him: "Would you really do that as a leader, or did you say that to impress me?"

"Maybe a little bit of both," he said, looking sheepish. "But I do have a question. If I started off saying something positive about their idea, with my goal of getting them to consider my idea instead, didn't I just weaken my position? I told them what I liked about their idea, but they haven't committed anything to my idea. What keeps them from saying, 'Well, if you like our ideas so much, let's go ahead with them'?"

Cynthia sipped her coffee. "Two things: good intention and trust."

"Good intention? Trusting that someone will support you? Do you think that works? Really, is that enough? You know, this reminds me of one time when I was at bat—the pitcher had thrown two fastballs into the dirt. I'm looking at 2 and 0. The catcher muttered, 'This guy can't throw a pitch today.' So

I figure I am going to get on base the easy way. I kept my bat on my shoulder. Guess what? Three fast balls down the middle. I'm out."

Cynthia bit her lip and considered whether this was the teachable moment, the opening she'd been waiting for to talk about his baseball clichés and analogies. Pulling her chair closer to the table, she leaned in. "I'm not sure I see the connection."

"Trust! I trusted him! I was wrong! The guy could throw! They set me up. Two in the dirt to make me think he didn't have it, and then three across the plate. He was—"

"Rafa," she said, "can I interrupt you for a minute? I just want to switch gears for a second." She paused, and then continued. "What's your relationship with your coworkers, in general? Aside from this issue, how do you get along with them? For example, do they know about your frustration at work? Do they share some of your same issues?"

Rafa lowered his eyes for a moment. "I'm sure they know I am frustrated. Listen, I've been there almost two years and they've all worked there for a lot longer. Yeah, I think we all want to be more involved in decision making. But I think most of them are content to just do the work and then go home."

"Not everyone wants to lead," said Cynthia. "But here's a related question. Do you have friends in your department? Who do you hang out with?"

Rafa shrugged. "Well, to be honest, I don't think we relate to each other. First of all, several of them are older women. They treat me like a son. And none of the guys are into baseball. I have tried to get a couple of them interested in going to a game with me, but I never seem to have any takers. Can you believe it? In this town?" He rolled his eyes.

Enough already about the baseball.

———————

Cynthia seized the moment and proceeded cautiously.

"Rafa," she began, "I am wondering: At work, do you do the baseball thing?"

Rafa looked mystified. "What baseball thing?"

"In the short time since we've known each other, I've heard you use baseball references in just about every situation you can. I know baseball was the focal point of your life. It was your goal, your passion, and your dream. I get that, and I'm sure others do too. But it's over and it has been over for, what, six years now?"

He nodded.

"So I'm wondering, with all the analogies, the stories, the achievements—it seems like it's still very much alive for you in your head. And I'm wondering if you have really moved on. Since this is a question I have, and I've only known you for four weeks, is it possible that others who work with you wonder as well? Maybe even Wally?"

Rafa hesitated. He felt embarrassed and a little exposed. "I didn't think it was so bad to tell stories or make analogies. I think sometimes it helps make things clearer. It does for me."

"Stories are great, Rafa. They help others better understand who we are. They show that we are open and willing to share. But the stories we choose to tell also communicate a message. Your stories, for example, are all about baseball. And most of them are stories about a time when you were a star—they always show your best side, your winning side. And you're talking baseball to people who really don't care about the game one way or the other. I wonder what message that sends to others."

Cynthia's comments met with dead silence. Rafa seemed to have shut down completely. She decided to give him time to ponder her comments. "So, what do you think? I really want to hear what you're thinking right now."

Rafa had clearly been caught off guard by her direct approach. "You're asking me what message am I sending others when I tell my baseball stories? I have to think about it." More silence followed. Rafa looked down at the floor.

Cynthia sensed he was uncomfortable and feeling vulnerable; she hoped he wasn't feeling under attack. She decided to give him some time to regroup. "I'm just going to get a refill. My jet lag needs more caffeine. I will be right back. Can I get you anything?"

Rafa shook his head.

When she sat down again with a new cup, he had his arms folded across his chest, but he was ready to talk. "OK, I guess one message is that you think I'm obsessed with baseball. And you obviously think it's getting in the way."

Cynthia leaned back in her chair and looked him directly in the eye. Rafa saw that she was waiting for more. "I guess it also might make people think that I'm stuck in the past. Like the big man on campus who's over the hill and always talking about his glory days. Is that what are you're thinking?" He started to relax a bit, less defensive and genuinely wanting to know.

"Well, that could be one take on it," said Cynthia. "But I can see another take too. Maybe your coworkers, including Wally, see it as a sign that you need to be the star—the best, the hero, the winner. On the other hand, you just told me a story about taking three called strikes. Do you ever tell stories like that to other people? Stories about when you lost the game for your team?"

Rafa didn't reply.

"Listen," she said, giving him what she hoped was a warm smile, "I enjoy the baseball talk. It's part of your personality, and you've have already taught me a thing or two about the game. But I suspect that it may be too much for your coworkers, day in and day out. And honestly, you are too young to be stuck in the past. You really don't want to put yourself out there as an ex-jock who is reliving his glory days."

Rafa looked pained. "I really don't want to be that guy."

"And yet you may appear to be like that."

"Great," said Rafa. "So what do I do?"

Instead of answering, she deflected the question. "What do you think would be a good start?"

"Nix the baseball talk."

This poor guy. She knew she'd had to address the issue head on—it was likely already affecting his relationships. But she could see that coming to this realization was painful. "Rafa, you don't need to stop talking about baseball totally. It means too much to you. Remember our discussion about right and wrong? It doesn't have to be all or nothing. Instead, put it in perspective. Use other stories, ones that relate to who you are now and what you are experiencing now. And be willing to talk about your mistakes. It shows people that you know you're human, and they are less apt to feel judged by you. In fact, they'll probably feel closer to you."

"Huh," said Rafa.

Cynthia changed track slightly. "You know, one thing that I found very helpful when I was trying to build some credibility in a new department was asking questions."

"Questions? How do questions build credibility? Isn't it just the opposite? Doesn't it show you don't know things?"

"Well, think about it. How do you feel when someone asks you a question about how to do something?"

Rafa paused for a moment. "Well," he said, "I guess it depends on who asks and what they ask me. Stupid questions just annoy me. But when someone asks me a hard question about how to do something, I feel like they think I am smart, that I am reliable."

"And if they think that you're smart, you might naturally be drawn to them—they obviously have good sense! Well, the same thing happens in reverse. If you ask one of your coworkers a question, or even Wally, you are saying, 'I think you are smart, so I want to know something you know.' Instead of your appearing invulnerable, they are drawn to you because you've paid them a compliment. And who doesn't like a compliment?"

"Oh, OK . . . I see how that works. Wow. I was trained a completely different way—like my entire life from age eight to twenty."

Cynthia was intrigued. "How was that?

"I was taught that asking for help was a sign of weakness. 'Don't expose your vulnerabilities. The competition will eat you alive.'"

So that's where his bravado comes from. "You know, Rafa, that may be true in competitive sports, and maybe it is a habit that's hard to break, but this isn't baseball—this is the business world. Yes, we deal with competition, but our everyday interactions are with our colleagues—our coworkers, not our competitors." She paused. "They aren't the enemy."

She took another sip of coffee to give Rafa a chance to absorb her comments. "I wonder if you have pushed people away because you have sent the message that they are the 'other side.' What do you think?"

Rafa was uncharacteristically quiet for several minutes. Cynthia began to think that she hadn't moved cautiously enough. Maybe she had pushed him too far, too fast. "Rafa," she said, "I'm not the enemy either."

Rafa looked up and caught her eye.

She smiled. "I'm on your side. We are on the same team. All of us at CTBN are your team members. And as team members, we need to know your strengths, and we also need to understand your challenges. We rely on you, so we need to know what we can and cannot expect from you. We aren't asking you to be perfect, and you don't have to be the superstar. We want you to use all your skills and talents to help CTBN be its best. We need you to access and use the help available to grow and develop so you can be your best self—that's why we're in this mentoring relationship, right? And we need you to help other people grow and learn what you already know. That's the deal."

"Yeah, OK . . ." Rafa was working to get his voice under control. Cynthia thought, *I really hit a nerve. But I think he's tough enough to course correct quickly.*

"I get it," Rafa continued, more strongly now. "I see what you mean. Chucking all the baseball talk is going to be tough, it's a lifelong habit . . . Would you remind me if I strike out?"

Cynthia winced.

"OK, OK—if I, uh, if I fall off the wagon?"

"Count on it. Remember, it's not fatal if you do. But if you begin to build stronger relationships with your coworkers, who knows? They might eventually like baseball if you met them halfway. Try to find out what they are interested in. Do that first, and maybe the other will follow."

"If I build it they will come? Sorry!" Rafa laughed. "Couldn't resist that one."

Cynthia was glad to see how resilient he was. But she was pretty sure they would still have some personality issues to deal with in the future.

"Oh, and Rafa, let me know about what you do with the issue with your team. I want to hear how you decide to handle it. You had some good ideas when you were the director of Strategic Planning Consulting a minute ago." She smiled. "Why not try and incorporate a few of his ideas? I think they will help."

Rafa looked up from his tablet, where he was furiously recording notes. "I will. I have to think about what might work. Lots and lots to think about."

"I think we have covered enough for today. Don't you?"

Rafa inhaled deeply and blew out a big breath of relief. "I'll say!"

"So how about if you summarize our discussion again and shoot it off in an email to me? And, of course, set an agenda for our next meeting. At our next meeting we can definitely talk about your presentation—it's scheduled for next week, right? I'll send you a few more questions to consider for our next meeting, to help you start to identify some goals. How does that sound?"

"Like we need more than an hour again," Rafa smiled.

Cynthia stood. "I have to go—piles of paper are waiting for me." She laughed. Then, serious, she said, "I think we took on some important issues this morning. I know it was a hard conversation, and I was a little hesitant about raising thorny issues so early in our relationship. I'm glad you were so receptive to them. It takes a certain level of maturity to be able to deal with challenging issues like these. I hope the meeting was helpful to you, and that in time you will feel it better prepared you to 'go the distance.'"

Rafa stood up too, extending his hand for a warm handshake. "Cynthia, it was . . . it really was helpful. You gave me a lot to think about, especially the baseball stuff. I hadn't understood how much it pushed people away. I was actually trying to use it for the opposite reason. So thank you for the feedback."

They walked out together and Cynthia waved goodbye. Rafa headed straight for his car at the far end of the lot. He exhaled deeply as he unlocked the door and dropped heavily into his seat. *Cynthia was right*, he thought. *This mentoring stuff is work.*

———————

As Rafa shifted his car into gear, he started to replay the session in his head. Cynthia had been pretty tough about his fixation on baseball, but he sensed kindness and caring behind her words. He could see how she'd gotten to her position in the company—she was a total professional. She'd warned him she was going to be candid, but it still hurt. He hated being criticized, and he didn't like feeling this way. But he couldn't stop thinking about what she'd told him.

Maybe she was right. Maybe he was still too caught up in the game. Did he really use baseball terms and analogies all the time? And was it really that important? Maybe it just annoyed her. Then again, her observations had gone deeper than baseball.

Did he really portray himself as the hero all the time? Were all his stories designed to make him look good? He really hadn't been conscious of doing that, but maybe she had a point. Nonno had always told him that it was as important to be a good winner as it was to be a good loser. That made him think that maybe he'd been a little too full of himself on the field, too. It hurt to think that Nonno might be disappointed in him.

The last thing Rafa wanted anyone—let alone Wally or his team—to think about him was that he was arrogant or boastful. *I am not that person.*

How had that even come up in their conversation? He'd been looking for some validation about his problem with his team's consistent pushback on his recommendations and some strategies for bringing his team over to his point of view. He'd just wanted her to say that he was right, but she wouldn't go there. She'd said that people didn't need to be always right or always wrong, and maybe he needed to ease up and be more positive and open to their input. And he'd actually come up with a solution to his problem himself. How had Cynthia gotten him to do that?

He freeze-framed the conversation. She'd asked him how he would handle the situation if he were the director. He had to come up with something in a hurry. In a flash, something he had learned in the NextGen Leadership Program about building bridges surfaced for him. At the time, he'd thought that "building bridges" was just an interesting academic exercise—he hadn't understood its practical realities until that very moment. *Whoa.*

He had to admit that when he laid it out for Cynthia, the concept made more sense. He started to think about how he could apply it with his team right now, in real time. Cynthia had given him a whole new perspective, and everything was starting to look different. His leadership was suddenly headed in a different direction. He needed to fix his problem quickly, so that he didn't embarrass himself in front of senior leaders and alienate his coworkers in the process. *If I am totally honest with myself, I want to be successful in front of Cynthia, too. I want her to be proud of me. I don't want to let her down.* It struck him that maybe this was the first test of their mentoring relationship. He wanted to pass.

OK, now he was committed to a quick solution. He needed to figure out his next steps with his team immediately. For the rest of the drive back to the office, he rehearsed what he would say to his teammates.

———————

Cynthia raced back to her office. She dropped her tote bag on the floor next to her desk and stared out the window. Normally, she would be thinking about the meeting she was about to facilitate, but she couldn't get her mind off the unexpectedly heavy conversation she had just had with Rafa.

She had intentionally slowed down, taking time to draw out Rafa's ideas about how he would approach his team. She could have easily told him how to handle it. She'd done it herself a million times. She was sure that he would have been fine with that, and it would have allowed them to cover more ground during the meeting. But she wasn't sure he really would have understood it on a deeper level. Anyway, efficiency wasn't the purpose of mentoring. Real learning, she knew, came from self-discovery, not from being told what to do.

She had felt a little bad about bringing up those never-ending baseball analogies—but really, almost one after the other! They had pushed her right to the edge. Clearly, he wasn't even aware of doing it. Maybe *why* he was doing it was something he was going to need to grapple with on his own. She wasn't going to be his therapist. But he needed to get a grip on it, and soon. If she had noticed the habit after only a couple of brief meetings and an email, she was almost positive that it was getting in the way of his effectiveness and relationships with his coworkers. And, knowing Wally, it must be driving him crazy too. Still, she thought of her son, and his endless sports references. She hoped she hadn't come down too hard on her mentee.

Cynthia decided to send Rafa a reassuring note along with some reflective questions for him to think about before the next meeting. She made a note to remind herself to follow up, and she added a reminder to ask Rafa about his presentation next week. Knowing that she had a plan in place to follow up with Rafa made her feel better. She turned her attention to her next meeting, grabbed her laptop, and walked out the door.

Later, after a very long day, Cynthia sat down and updated her calendar with all the upcoming commitments she had made that day. The meeting she had attended not only hadn't gone well but also had unexpectedly lasted most of the day. And now she had several command performance cross-country trips to make.

One of them would conflict with the next scheduled meeting with Rafa, and she wanted to let him know immediately. She launched her email program and sent him a note about rescheduling. "Just got several trips put on my calendar. I need to reschedule our mentoring meeting. Will get back with some suggested times."

Rafa opened the email from Cynthia as soon as it arrived in his inbox. He was disappointed to read that she was cancelling the meeting, and just when he most needed her support. He knew that things pop up, but he didn't trust that this was one of those times. He thought back on their meeting earlier in the day and wondered if what they talked about had any bearing on the cancellation. Had she lost interest in mentoring him? Had she given up on him so soon? Did the baseball thing bother her that much? He shot back a neutral reply.

After four days, when Rafa still hadn't heard back from Cynthia, he started to stew. She was busy, but still . . . His mind kept going back to their meeting, and then her cancellation. He thought about sending another email, but didn't want to be intrusive or appear needy.

He decided to man up and focus positive energy on creating strategies for improving his relationship with his coworkers and coming up with a set of strategically focused recommendations to present on Wednesday—just a week away. He tried to be more conscientious about eliminating baseball references from his vocabulary. Now that he was more aware of them, he realized that they *were* pretty frequent.

———————

The reminder about following up with Rafa popped up on Cynthia's calendar just as Rafa was due to give his presentation. Her heart sank when she saw it. *Damn it.* She had never gotten back to him to reschedule their mentoring meeting. She had broken one of the cardinal rules of their relationship. It was too late to pick up the phone.

She decided to instead work her way over to Rafa's department on the other side of the building. Rafa wasn't there, of course, nor were most of the employees from finance—they were all at the presentation. Fortunately, it was relatively easy to find his cubicle—it seemed to represent him perfectly. Right in the center of the corkboard was a newspaper clipping of Cal Ripken, Jr., fielding a ground ball. Although the picture was black and white, tattered, and somewhat blurry, you could still see that Ripken's eyes were completely focused and intent on the ball speeding toward him. And right in the center of the board was a photograph of an elderly man with his arm around a young boy wearing a Red Sox cap and a baseball mitt.

Rafa's desk was orderly. Clearly, he had been working hard on the presentation—various colored sticky notes were neatly arranged in topic order on his white board. Borrowing one of the many pens in the coffee cup by his phone, Cynthia scribbled a quick note of apology for not getting back to him sooner and added, "Stopped by to see you. Good luck on your presentation. Looking forward to hearing about how it went. Are you available for a meeting next Wednesday afternoon in my office? 2–3 or 4–5? Cynthia."

———————

Walking back to his office after the presentation, Rafa was flying high. He had scored a big one. His coworkers had high-fived him, and people he didn't know told him how well the presentation had gone. Even Wally had shaken his hand and told him he had done a "sterling" job.

When he returned to his desk, he saw Cynthia's note and immediately grabbed it up. He couldn't believe that she had come to his office space to apologize, and he was surprised at how relieved he felt. Between the presentation and the note from Cynthia, he felt like he just hit a walk-off home run. He decided to keep that last thought to himself.

Rafa was eager to share all of the positive feedback he had received on his presentation with Cynthia. After all, she was partly responsible for his success in bringing his coworkers on board. He couldn't wait to give her the blow-by-blow description. So when he opened an email from Cynthia on Thursday, he was pumped. But then he came down to earth. More work, apparently.

Cynthia confirmed the time that Rafa had chosen for their meeting, but requested that they meet at her office again instead of the café. Then she asked him to think about six questions in preparation for their discussion:

1. What skills and talents are you utilizing on the job?
2. What skills and talents are you underutilizing?
3. What is your Achilles' heel?
4. Where do you see as your biggest need for growth and development?
5. What would help raise your competence level?
6. What would raise your confidence level as a leader?

Rafa read the questions several times. It looked like he had some heavy preparation ahead of him. He hoped they'd have time for a little celebration.

Digging Deeper

Questions for Mentors:

1. In preparation for his mentoring meetings, Rafa allocates a specific time period for each agenda item. What are the advantages to doing this? What are the disadvantages?

2. In thinking about your mentoring meetings, what topics do you typically cover? Do you allocate time for connecting, checking in on current issues, and discussing progress on goals?

3. Cynthia confronts Rafa on an issue that she believes is getting in his way, and she is fairly blunt in her approach. What do you think of how Cynthia handled the baseball issue with Rafa? What did she do well? What would you do differently?

4. Have you ever had to give hard feedback to your mentees about a behavior that was getting in the way for you? How did it go? What could you have done differently to improve the outcome?

5. Rafa notices that Cynthia doesn't give him the answer to a question, but asks probing questions that help him come up with his own answer. What are the benefits for the mentee? What are the benefits for the mentor?

6. How comfortable and effective are you at asking your mentees probing questions that make them discover their own answers? What strategies can you use to ensure your effectiveness in this area?

7. How do you record and keep track of your mentoring conversations so that you can manage them?

Questions for Mentees:

1. In preparation for his mentoring meetings, Rafa allocates a specific time period for each agenda item. What are the advantages to doing this? What are the disadvantages?

2. In thinking about your mentoring meetings, what topics would be important to cover? How much time would you allocate for connecting with your mentor, checking in on current issues, and discussing progress on goals?

3. Cynthia confronts Rafa about an issue that she believes is getting in his way, and she is fairly blunt in her approach. What do you think of how Cynthia handled the baseball issue with Rafa? What worked well and what would you have wanted her to do differently?

4. Have you ever received hard feedback from your mentor about something you were doing that was getting in your way? How did it go? How did you respond? Is there anything you could have done or said that would have added value to the experience?

5. Rafa notices that Cynthia doesn't give him the answer to a question, but asks probing questions to help him come up with his own answer. What are the advantages to her approach?

6. Even though giving answers is the easiest and fastest way to get from point A to point B, mentees learn more when they grapple with issues and come up with their own answers. Some mentees are more comfortable than others with this approach. What is your comfort level with it? What might your mentor say or do to stimulate your thinking about issues?

The Fourth Meeting: Sorting It Out

As Rafa rode the elevator up to Cynthia's office, he thought about all that had happened since their last session. He'd been super busy and productive, doing the hard work of engaging the team in the collaborative work of preparing the presentation and then helping him hone his delivery. Every time he thought about how well that meeting had gone, he smiled. But then he thought about the questions Cynthia had sent him, and he found himself shaking his head. She'd really thrown him a curve ball—reflection was just not his thing. *But wait until I tell her about the progress I've made in curbing my baseball-speak,* he thought, brightening.

Cynthia straightened up her desk. She had barely had time to breathe between meetings today, but she was looking forward to seeing Rafa, especially after yesterday's casual lunchtime conversation. She'd run into Paul Gee, an executive from finance, who had sat in on Rafa's presentation and was extremely positive about it.

"That presentation was something else."

"Really? How so?" Cynthia had asked.

"Well, the numbers look good," Paul explained, "and the young man who presented the projections and recommendations for expenditure allocations for the next fiscal year—Moretti?—was very impressive. Poised, confident, thoughtful."

Then, unbidden, he launched into a play-by-play of the meeting. "That kid is fast on his feet. Man, was I impressed. When Tony Max challenged him—as only our COO can do—with his notorious 'So, what's the flaw in your recommendation?' question, he didn't fall into the trap like some of our ambitious young guys do."

Cynthia rolled her eyes. "I've been on the receiving end of that one too. Ouch. So how did he respond?"

"Pretty handily. He said, 'There are a number of flaws in our recommendations if certain assumptions don't pan out. For example, if our revenue growth fails to stay on the current course or if there is a truck strike and we can't deliver product. And, of course, if our biggest customer goes out of business.'"

"And what did Tony say?"

"He narrowed his eyes and said, 'Good answer.'"

Cynthia said, "It doesn't get better than that with Tony, does it?" and they both laughed.

"Why are you so interested in a kid from finance?" Paul asked. "Does he work for you?"

Cynthia shook her head. "No," she said, "we are working together on something."

Rafa arrived right on time and was promptly escorted into Cynthia's office. As he sat down across from her, she inched a bowl of individually wrapped dark chocolates toward him. "This is my afternoon treat. Want to join me?"

Rafa smiled and shook his head. "No thanks. I never got into sweets."

"Lucky you," Cynthia said. "It's my downfall."

Rafa almost said, "It doesn't seem to show," but thought better of it. That was definitely not the tone of this relationship. Instead, he pulled out his agenda and his tablet and looked up. "You know," he said, "I want to thank you for the note you left last week. I was beginning to get concerned when I received your email about the cancellation and there were no follow-up dates. I thought maybe I was getting dumped."

"That was really a case of 'my bad,'" Cynthia acknowledged. "I sent the first email, but then everything went into a black hole, and I completely forgot to send follow-up dates. When I realized my mistake, I ran down to your office. I felt terrible, so I wanted to apologize in person." She paused. "Enough mea culpa. I can't wait to hear about the presentation. I am all ears. Start from the beginning and tell me how you got your team on board."

"It was awesome," he said, enthusiastic in a way that Cynthia hadn't seen from him before. Rafa spent the next ten minutes describing how he met one-on-one with a few of his coworkers. He talked about the value of the various ideas that were currently on the table and about how he finally got them to agree to a meeting to flesh out the best of the ideas and take the presentation to the next level.

"I couldn't believe how well they responded," he said. "And they seem to have loosened up with me. I wouldn't say we're all best friends, but we're definitely getting along better day to day." *Except for Ted*, he thought, but shook it off. As he told Cynthia his story, he disciplined himself to make sure that his comments about his coworkers were positive.

"That's huge progress in just a couple of weeks," Cynthia said. "And what was the outcome? How did you think your presentation went?"

"I thought it went really well," he smiled, stopping himself from adding *I hit a home run.* "We did our homework, and it was pretty thorough. Even Wally congratulated me." Rafa was beaming now.

The shift from "I" to "we" in Rafa's language did not go unnoticed by Cynthia. Rafa was a quick study. "Well," she said, "I can confirm that you made quite an impression with the executives. I heard you handled the COO's bait very well."

"Was that what it was?" Rafa asked. "I didn't know it was bait. I thought it was a legitimate question. I just handled it as best I could."

"Well, you proved that you're fast on your feet and a good thinker, which earns big points with this crowd. Good for you." She paused to take another chocolate. "So, with all of that—the team, the baseball stuff, the presentation—what are the big lessons for you from a leadership perspective?"

"Well, for one thing, I got your message about right or wrong. I have been careful not to use those words with other people. And it's actually funny how often I had to catch myself before saying, 'You're wrong' or 'That's not right.' You've got me thinking more about how I would react to those kinds of judgmental comments. I don't like being wrong. And I don't like someone telling me I am wrong. And I don't want to be that guy with other people."

Rafa stared out the window, trying to figure out how much more he should share with Cynthia. "I'm not going to say something I don't believe," he began. "Like, I'm not going to say 'Great idea!' when I actually think it's weak. But I am trying to be more thoughtful about how I communicate my position. You know, like that quote you mentioned, 'Begin with the end in mind'? Well, that stuck with me. It is a really helpful reminder."

"In what way?"

"Well, just yesterday, I thought about it before I started a conversation with my coworkers about our new project. I think I did a better job starting out on the right foot this time because I did start with the end in mind to get them all on board early. So I acknowledged the team's ideas first, and pointed out the suggestions that I honestly thought we could work with, and that started them really getting excited about the project. They were on board from the beginning, and they were actively working with me instead of just sitting there. And I felt more like part of the group too, instead of an outsider, which is a change. So, great quote. Thanks!"

Cynthia was pleased to hear that he was applying what he learned and that it seemed to be working for him. It also pleased her that he was being so conscientious, and that their mentoring conversations were already making a difference for him. "You are very welcome. Anything else from last time?"

Rafa thought for a minute. "You know, this week I finally saw the value of the mentoring."

Cynthia was surprised. "I didn't think you were dragged in here kicking and screaming. Explain, please."

Rafa turned beet red. Had he insulted her? "No, you're right—a lot of people told me I'd benefit from mentoring, and you know I really want to get ahead in this organization. But I confess, I wasn't sure how it was going to work, what it would be, how it would help, where I would go with it—I thought it would be just 'coaching,' like you said. And then it turned out that mentoring was way different from that, and it kind of threw me."

He looked at Cynthia to see how she was taking this, but she was just listening, as usual, and seemed interested. He forged ahead: "But this week, for the first time, I really wanted to talk to you about how things came down last week with the presentation. Bounce the feedback off of you, hear your thoughts, good or bad. There isn't a place for me to take any of that. I certainly don't see myself sitting down with Wally to talk about what I'm feeling, things I'm uncertain of, what I'm learning from all of this. He would never have that kind of conversation with me, and I would never initiate it with him. I'm not sure why this mentoring thing makes it work so well. But for some reason, in this setting, I feel really comfortable doing it."

Cynthia was pleased to hear this. "Rafa, I think it has something to do with feeling safe. Remember, we talked about that early on? It's just you and me, and it's not going past me. You don't have to worry how it will sound to someone who essentially signs your paycheck or conducts your performance review or puts your name up for a promotion. And it's starting to make me see how strong a constraint that can be. In fact, it made me think more about my own team."

"Really?" Rafa was surprised that there was something about leadership she hadn't realized until now.

"Yes, I don't think I fully understood it before, but I'm starting to wonder about how much my direct reports might edit themselves in front of me. None of my folks currently have mentors, so they don't have a sounding board—they just have me. And while of course I am a great boss"—she smiled—"I can see that it's really not as safe for them to be completely open and honest as I wish it could be. Our conversations together have helped me with that realization. So thank you for that."

"Well, I guess, you're welcome. Even if I didn't know I was helping you. But I agree. I do feel safe. I feel comfortable being able to say what I need to say here. It's too bad it's the only place I can do it. But I am glad at least I have that."

"So is there anything else you have on your agenda before we hit the questions?" Cynthia asked.

"No, that's it. But I did want to let you know that our NextGen group is having a meeting next month. It's called a Roundtable—they want each of us to give an update on where we're at with our mentoring and what we're doing with our mentors. Should be interesting to hear what's happening with the others."

"Ah," said Cynthia, "that will be interesting. I look forward to hearing how it goes."

"No fears, I'll share it all," Rafa laughed.

"Okay, then. Let's get started."

———

Rafa flipped through pages on his tablet for a minute and finally found the notes he was looking for. "This was a tough assignment."

"How so?"

"Really? Cynthia. These questions are killers. 'What skills and talents am I utilizing on the job? What am I underutilizing? What's my Achilles' heel? Where is my biggest need for growth and development? What would help raise my competence level? What would raise my confidence level?' These are not simple questions."

"No, they're not. But they are important questions for us to tackle because the answers are important for you to understand.

I want to make sure that you feel more competent and confident in a leadership role. That's important, because you can move forward with strength only when you aren't second-guessing yourself. If you don't understand where you are strong and where you need to improve, you could inadvertently shoot yourself in the foot. For example, your resistance to answering the questions tells me that maybe you're not comfortable with self-reflection, or maybe you just think it takes too much work, or maybe you tend to be dismissive of things you don't see the point of right away, or—"

"OK, OK," said Rafa, holding up his hands in surrender. "I think I see where this is going."

But Cynthia wasn't done. "You need to know your strengths because you need to be leveraging your strengths. If you have a talent you aren't tapping into, it's a wasted resource, right? So let's make identifying your strengths our first priority. It is the easiest, and it's positive. Then we can look at the flip side—the gap analysis, your weaknesses, the areas that might most adversely affect your performance. And then your Achilles' heel tells us what your blind sides are. Of course that's probably the hardest to identify, by definition."

"Good point," Rafa said. "That's kind of the story of my life. It's hard to know. I'm always so sure I'm right. Is that my blind side?" He saw Cynthia smiling, but he couldn't read her. "Plus, even if I think I know what my strengths are, I'm not sure Wally agrees with me."

"I found myself in a similar situation once. I thought I was pretty good at strategic vision and planning, and I kept pushing my boss to put me on one of those high-powered teams that led the strategy charge. My boss finally sat down with me and told me he didn't think I had yet acquired the necessary experience and skills that would entitle me to work with senior leadership. I was disappointed with the feedback—it didn't fit my image of myself at all. And I certainly didn't welcome the rejection. Fortunately, he saw some potential, and he was willing to help me find a way to get the experience I needed to be able to get where I want to go."

"So are you saying I should ask Wally for feedback about my skill sets? See what he says?"

"It's a place to start. It will give us *one* perspective. And it might actually line up with yours. If it doesn't, maybe Wally can help you gain the experience you need to get where you want to go."

"Maybe that would help. But I have to confess, I feel totally out of my element walking into Wally's office and asking for feedback. I get it that maybe I would finally know where I stand with him, but the whole situation seems unnatural, stilted, and uncomfortable. He was pretty pleased about my presentation last week, though, so maybe it won't be too bad . . ." Rafa drifted into thought, his brow furrowed. He was hoping Cynthia would let him off the hook here.

"Why don't we start out by getting your own perspective on yourself—how you see you? Then you can bring that knowledge to your talk with Wally down the line. What do you think?"

"Okay, sure. I guess you're not just going to tell me my strengths and weaknesses and let me get back to work. And I guess that's really not what I'm here for, so . . ." Rafa looked at his tablet. "First question, what skills and talents am I utilizing on the job?"

Cynthia waited.

Rafa started counting off on his fingers. "One, I would say I am pretty good at critical thinking. Two, I think I am good—"

"Wait a second, Rafa," Cynthia interrupted. "Before you move on, I have a question. How do you define 'critical thinking'? I just want to make sure we're on the same page."

"Huh. Well, to me, it's about listening to someone describe a fairly complex issue or a problem and being able to dissect it down to the core. Asking the kinds of questions that help drill down past the biases, emotions, and subjectivity, and eventually being able to offer up an overview of the problem, some reasoned conclusions, and possible solutions. That, to me, is critical thinking."

As he described the issue, Cynthia saw a maturity in him that she hadn't seen before. It was the same side Paul must have seen in him during his presentation. "Well said. That's my assessment too. What else are your strong points?"

"Understanding the financial implications of a problem is a part of it. I'm pretty good at analyzing the numbers and making sense of them, or seeing the holes. I enjoy analyzing numbers as they relate to business projections. For me, it is pure fun."

"That's amazing. Spreadsheets are anything but fun for me. I am glad someone enjoys it, and I am glad it is you."

Rafa paused to see if Cynthia was waiting for more from him. She had her head down and was taking notes, and he couldn't tell. He decided to keep going. "And I think I'm also pretty good at giving presentations. I can stand up in front of a group and speak coherently. At least they don't see my knees shaking, thank God." He chuckled to himself.

"So were you nervous during the presentation last week?"

"My first presentation in front of senior leaders? What do you think? God, yes. But I can still do it and not let people know I'm shaking inside. I think that's what counts. I'm hoping that if I do it enough, the nerves will subside."

"They will. I used to be as nervous as you are right now, at least in the beginning. Over time, though, as I got more experience under my belt, speaking and presenting became more familiar, more comfortable. I felt more confident in my abilities and in what I had to say and less like I needed to prove myself. Lots of things contributed to my nervousness, but it definitely became easier over time. Though I can still get a little anxious ahead of time, depending on the situation."

Knowing that Cynthia was able to overcome her presentation challenges was a relief, and Rafa appreciated her frankness. She didn't posture or pretend to be perfect, yet she was an incredibly confident and capable leader.

Cynthia reviewed her notes. "Okay, good. This is a solid list. So those are the skills you are utilizing at work. How about additional skills you have that you *aren't* drawing on—the ones that you're underutilizing but that you want to do more of?"

"Well, personally, I see myself as strong at problem solving— maybe that involves critical thinking? I can listen to issues and cut to the chase and pretty quickly develop a path to a solution. But I get zero chance at that in Wally's department. Not much collaboration there—what we did on the presentation was pretty much a first. And the same is true about negotiating. I think I am pretty good at it. But I don't get to do much of it in my current position."

"Good ones," she said, still taking notes. "Problem solving, negotiating—those are very important skills for leaders. Now, how about the deficit side? That's our next question, right?"

"What's my Achilles' heel?" Rafa laughed. "I can relate to that question on many levels."

"Well, let's keep it to the business level," Cynthia said.

"I guess it's that my baseline assumption is that I'm right, so it's hard for me to see that I may not be. That's gotten me in trouble recently, as you know." They both laughed.

"That's a good one to try to keep in mind so you don't get blindsided again," said Cynthia. "So how about the areas that you really need to work on?"

"Well, collaboration is a new skill for me. I haven't been so successful collaborating with my team—until last week, of course. And that was with advice from you that had never even crossed my mind. And I want to be a better listener, but that is definitely not my strength. I tend to just want to get to the next thing I had in mind to talk about."

Cynthia smiled.

"Yeah . . ." Rafa was struck by a memory. "I loved how my grandfather listened to me, like I was the most important person he knew. But *I* haven't mastered that one yet. I think you can already see that I tend to push my own opinion, probably too hard for most. I've been told that before. People get intimidated and put off. So that's another one. And I'm impatient. Obviously.

I get frustrated when things move too slowly. I'm not good at waiting for other people to catch up, or get on board with it, or even get it. So, that's four things. Do I need more?"

"Four's just fine." Cynthia said. "I think you did a nice job of self-assessment after all. Now we have to figure out what to do with all this!"

———————

Cynthia put down her pencil. "Rafa, if you were going to focus on some leadership development areas, would you prefer to work on leveraging your strengths or on addressing some of your challenges?"

"I don't know—it's a little overwhelming to think about."

"Okay, let me put it this way: Which would be more helpful to you?"

"That's a good question. I guess the real question for me is, which of those things is the most important for me to bring to the table if I want to advance myself? It might be helpful if I knew what CTBN has in mind for me. If I knew what kinds of positions and options were coming, I would be able to pick the skills I think I would need to work on. What do you think?"

"Honestly? That sounds like tackling the question from the wrong end."

Rafa looked blank.

"Rafa, are you asking what I think the company has in mind for you or what skills I think you should work on?"

"Well, of course, it's just that if I knew, or you knew, the possibilities down the road, that would be great. But I'm guessing you don't know, and the company isn't thinking about me in those terms. Am I right?"

"That's a pretty good guess. And I'm not sure that leadership qualities include molding yourself to someone else's needs."

"Oh, man. That hurts." *She must really think I'm a jerk.* Rafa was silent, thinking some more. "So, the question that's left is, what do you think are the skills a good leader needs, that match up with things that I need to work on?"

"Closer," said Cynthia, "but I think the better question may be, what do *you* want for you? And that is something you need to figure out for yourself."

She paused. Rafa seemed to be at a loss. So she went on, "Rafa, that said, here's a hint—there is no way a leader can be effective without continuously working on building relationships. One of the most helpful insights I got as I started to lead people was that you can't get anything to happen if others are not on board. The best ideas get shelved if no one is going to support them. Or worse, people sabotage your idea on purpose when they don't feel included. Either way, you end up losing, and a good idea is lost.

"You are off to a good start with your team. So if it were me, I would want to jump on that momentum. Why not look at items on your list that relate to engaging others? Which of the items on your list do you think accomplish that?"

Rafa was beginning to see a pattern in Cynthia's questioning. When he asked her a question, she had a way of turning it around on him so that he had to answer for himself. *My head hurts with all this.* "Okay, Cynthia, I get it. You're not going to give me the answers."

He smiled at her, but Cynthia waited without speaking. He was so close. If she just waited him out, she knew he'd come out with it.

"Well, in that case," Rafa said, staring at the wall for inspiration, "I guess I would start with listening. I think people are more likely to get on board if someone is listening to their ideas." He turned back to Cynthia: "Do you agree with that?"

"I do indeed! I think you are absolutely right. There are a lot of payoffs that come from listening. I have found, for example, that when I take the time to listen to what people are actually saying I have a clearer sense of where they're coming from—I understand their issues better. And I also find that if I listen to them, they are more likely to listen to me. Do you know what I mean?"

Rafa nodded.

"Your grandfather was a really good listener, right?"

"Oh, Nonno. Yeah, yeah, he was a master at it." Rafa relaxed a little. "So I would be sitting on the back porch, all glum and mad. Maybe I had made a mistake. Maybe I had blown our lead. Maybe I had made an error. He just listened. He never tried to talk me out of my position. In fact, sometimes he would agree with some 'sorry for myself' statement I made. Whatever he did, he got me to move on and think about turning it around next time. It always seemed to work. I know I always felt better."

"Pay attention to that example from your grandfather. There is a lot to learn from him." She let that sink in for a moment.

"So, listening." Cynthia jotted it in her notes. "That's one. What else?"

Rafa stared at the wall again. "I guess it is sort of related, but I tend to push my position even though I know it turns off some people. I have great ideas"—Cynthia chuckled at that, and Rafa grinned—"and it frustrates me when someone doesn't get them. I just won't give up. I keep trying to find another way to get them to agree. It often leads to an argument."

"Why do you have to push so hard? Where does that come from?" Cynthia waited, but Rafa could only shrug and shake his head. "Are you afraid that if you don't push your idea, someone else's idea will trump yours? And then you will be on the defensive?"

"No, I don't think so. I just want to make sure that whatever we do, we do it the right way."

"And yet you have a need to be right as well. Why has that become so important to you, Rafa?"

"Who wants to be wrong?" Rafa snapped. "But, yes, I do like being right. Is there anything wrong with that?" He folded his arms across his chest.

"No," Cynthia replied. "But I am wondering why things have to come down to right and wrong with you. And why being wrong is a no-go area for you."

"Maybe I'm not making myself clear. Or—OK," he said, exhaling. "I haven't really ever thought that was how I was seeing it. Is that how I'm coming across? I don't know why. I guess it has always been . . . like in baseball—sorry, but this is my life here—it's about making the A team. They post the list after tryouts. Even when they put everyone on the team, there is always the A team and the B team—the A team is the first column, the group with the best players, and that's the right list to be on. There's no future for the guys on the B team, and everyone knows it. That's what I try to do. I try to be on the best team."

"So pushing your idea is the same as pushing yourself to make the A team? Proving you're the best?"

Rafa sighed. "I didn't think about it that way, but I guess so. I . . . think so."

"There is nothing wrong with working toward being the best. That's what we try to do in business. Be the best. But when it becomes something more than striving to be the best, it goes over the top and out of leadership territory because all of a sudden it's less about the work and more about you. What do you think?

"I don't know. Early on, a lot of people went to bat for me." Realizing what he'd just said, he interrupted himself. "Oh, man, sorry. I just mean that a lot of people worked hard for me in those days. My parents sacrificed a lot for me to play ball. I had always thought I would be able to pay them back when I went pro. I didn't want to disappoint them."

"So, Rafa, it sounds to me like maybe you associate your idea or your position with *you*. If someone rejects your idea or doesn't take your position, it means they don't like *you*—you didn't make the team. Is that how you feel?"

Rafa leaned back in his chair. "Crap. Is that how it looks? Well, when you say it like that—yes. I think that's right." He blinked hard and shook his head.

"Do you see how that can get in the way for other people? No one is allowed to have an idea or opinion that's different from yours. And take it further—if you were leading a team, how could your team members ever disagree with you? You'd end up being a team of one. Then, who do you actually end up leading?" She paused. Rafa looked tense.

"By taking differing opinions personally," she explained, "you're bringing a whole new level of tension to any discussion. You clearly did a great job with your coworkers on the presentation, but one good experience isn't usually enough to change a deep-rooted, lifelong approach. And I think it's getting in your way. I think if you want to move forward, maybe it's time you get out of your own way."

"I didn't see it like that. I didn't realize I was making it personal. I certainly don't want to do that. But how do I fix it? It's kind of hard to just say I won't do that anymore. It's like a natural response. Obviously."

"Even if it's hard, it doesn't mean you can't do it. Look how well you're doing at becoming aware of the baseball analogies. Speaking of which, didn't you say you couldn't hit a pitch if it was up and away?"

"I thought we weren't using baseball stories anymore." Then he saw Cynthia's smile.

She continued, "Like I said before, sometimes it fits. I'm thinking that if you had to learn how to hit that pitch, maybe you would get in the batting cage?"

"A few hours, that's for sure."

"So then you'd hit a bunch of practice pitches, and maybe there would be someone giving you help on the side. I bet eventually you could learn to hit that pitch. This is the same thing, Rafa."

"OK. So listening is one thing I am going to work on, and the other is not making my ideas about me. Not taking it personally. Is that right?"

"Yes, that's right. So far, we've got two good starter goals. But we need to frame them in such a way that they are SMART goals.

Otherwise, they will be too broad—we need to have some tangible ways to measure your success." Cynthia paused. "Do you know the SMART model?"

"Sure," Rafa said immediately. "We worked with the SMART model in NextGen. It stands for specific, measurable, action-oriented, realistic, and, uh, timely. Right?"

"That's it. That way, you know what to work on and that whatever you do is getting the results you want. Do you see what I mean?"

"Yes, but—listening? How do you measure that?"

"Well, not just by saying, 'I'm listening' and checking off a box. That's not going to do it. Think: if we were trying to raise your proficiency at listening, what specifically would you be doing to show you are a better listener? How would others know you are listening?"

Rafa stared at the carpet, trying to visualize it. "Well," he began, "I'd say that you have a real talent for listening. And I am not saying that to flatter you. You make me feel like you are listening all the time."

"Well, good. Believe me, it's not a natural talent. It's a discipline, and I have to constantly work on it. Sometimes my enthusiasm gets the better of me, and I do more talking than listening."

Rafa smiled.

"So tell me, Rafa, how do you know I am listening to you? What are the indicators?"

"Well, for one thing, you never interrupt, which I do more than I like. How do you keep from doing that?"

"I try and stay in the moment, to be attentive to what you are saying to me without thinking ahead to what I'm going to say. That takes work. Most of us care more about our own ideas than the other person's ideas. But if you are trying to avoid jumping in on their words, you have to keep your own ideas out of your head."

Cynthia paused as Rafa took notes.

"Let me suggest that you do some thinking about those two goals in terms of the SMART model, Rafa—five great ways to tighten your goal. Why don't you try writing the goals, using that model to frame them, and send me what you come up with later this week?"

Rafa made a note in his tablet: "SMART goals."

"And, Rafa, one very important thing—this assignment is going to involve some reflection on your part. You should be asking yourself the question: Why is this goal important to my development? If it's not meaningful for you, then you won't have the motivation you need to accomplish it."

Rafa made a note: "Why it's important to my development." "That sounds like a plan. I'm probably going to need some help from you on this one. I'm not a journalist like you."

Cynthia glanced at her notes. "So where were we on those questions? You did 'underutilizing' and you did 'Achilles' heel,' weaknesses. How about any areas where others see you need growth and development?"

Rafa shrugged.

"Okay, you received 360-feedback during the NextGen Leadership training, yes? And surely you have had a performance review this last year. So what did those two pieces of feedback pinpoint? What did they tell you were leadership development needs?"

The afternoon sunlight bouncing off Camelback Mountain distracted Rafa for a moment. Someday he'd have an office with a view, he hoped. He turned away from the window. "The 360 was hard to figure out. I didn't really get much value from it."

"Really? I'm surprised—360s are usually extremely helpful in revealing performance gaps and areas of consensus. It gives you an opportunity to compare your perspective with those of your supervisor, peers, and direct reports. I'm a great believer in them."

"Well, mine wasn't so helpful. And it was a downer, basically. I didn't get what I was hoping for, that was for sure. People just didn't get me. For whatever reason, they dinged me big time. I was pretty surprised." He had an expression on his face that she hadn't seen before: sad.

"What did they say?"

Rafa closed his eyes briefly. "They said I dismissed them and disregarded them, and that I was disrespectful and uncooperative. That's just not how I see myself." He looked tired.

Cynthia noted the sudden change in mood and took care to be patient and sensitive with her response. "Well, let's look at it from a different perspective. A minute ago you told me that you weren't a good listener, you push your ideas, you need to win, and you don't collaborate as a team member. Those were your words. So when you ask your colleagues to comment on your leadership style, would you be surprised that they would be critical?"

"Probably not. But it wasn't my intention to do any of that, and they should have known it."

"Rafa, how is someone else supposed to understand your 'intention'? All they see is what you actually do. We judge ourselves by our own good intention, and others by their behavior. Have you ever heard that one? I don't know who said it, but it's true." Cynthia sat back and folded her arms.

"Yeah, I guess I do that," said Rafa. He repeated the quote several times and noted it in his tablet. He just wanted to hold it together until the end of the session.

"We all do it, Rafa, but in your case it is really working against you. You've been doing some things that people don't like, and they are drawing some not-so-flattering conclusions about those behaviors. Basically, you've been dismissing the fact that they find you dismissive. You may have had a legitimate intention, but what you intend to do doesn't show up in your behavior."

"Damn. Damn. Damn." Rafa was quietly banging his right fist into his left palm. "So how do I turn that around? I might as well move to another company if that's how people are seeing me."

Cynthia tried to reassure him. "Whoa, hold on. Rafa, that's what we are here for. That's why you have a mentor. We are going to do this together. It isn't impossible, I assure you. You can do it—you have already started, remember? You met with your team. You looked for ways to collaborate. And you made the first most important step with them: you expressed your intention at the outset. Remember, 'Begin with the end in mind'? Well, in your case, it is very helpful to start out declaring your intention. People are less likely to make assumptions based solely on your behaviors. See what I mean?"

"I see. That is exactly what I did with the team last week. I did start out telling them what I wanted to happen. That did seem to help."

"And apparently you changed their assessment of you toward the positive end a bit, right? So it is possible, and you already know how. If I were you, I'd keep doing that, Rafa. It will make a big difference."

Rafa looked like he'd gone ten rounds, but they still had some time left on the clock and she had some more points to make. Cynthia pushed the bowl of chocolates toward him again, and this time he took one.

———

Cynthia cautiously approached the topic of the performance review Rafa had recently received from Wally. "Let's move on—what feedback did you get from Wally?"

"Actually," Rafa said, "Wally was very complimentary about a lot of my skills. He tends to focus on the financial analysis component of the job and the technical skills. He didn't offer much by way of team stuff, the people thing, or leadership. So I really don't know how he sees me there."

"Do you think it matters, Rafa?"

"I'm guessing by your question that you think it does."

"Well. He is your boss. If you want a job promotion, or a job transfer, or anything in this company, he is going to influence the decision. There is no getting around that. It's to your benefit to know where you stand with him."

"OK. So what do I do?" Rafa asked.

"How about asking him?"

Rafa was caught off guard by her direct response. "Are you joking? Like walk in and say, 'Wally, what do you think of me?'"

Cynthia chose her words carefully. "Well, not exactly. Your approach needs to be a little more focused and directed, I would think."

"Then what do I say? Because my palms are starting to sweat just imagining this conversation."

"Are you afraid of what he will say?"

"Probably, a little—no, a lot. I mean, I told you about the 360. And it just seems so awkward. I'm not asking for a date. It's just kind of weird, isn't it?"

"From where I sit, Rafa, it isn't as weird as you think. For example, I personally like it when one of my people comes in and says something like, 'Can you give me an idea of how you think I am doing? Am I on track or is there something I need to work on?' I really appreciate the opportunity to hold that conversation—in fact, I encourage it. It tells me that the person really cares about the job, about improving in the job, and about what I think as their supervisor so maybe they can course correct. All of which makes me feel good about them."

"I never thought of it from that perspective," said Rafa.

"Yes, and it makes it a lot easier for me to be able to offer up some constructive criticism, because that is when they are most open and receptive—they are literally asking to hear it. I always try to say some positive things about their performance, and then identify some areas I want them to focus on. There are no surprises. They hear some positive things that make them feel good, so they know that I am on their side. And they have more confidence that they are working on the right things—they know what to focus on for improvement."

"Well, yeah, that's awesome, it really is. But Wally is not you."

Cynthia shrugged. "I've known Wally a long time. You might be surprised."

Rafa looked doubtful. "Maybe. OK, I'm game. So how do I get started? 'Knock, knock, Wally. Can you tell me what I need to work on?'"

"Well," she said with a smile, "how about something a little less abrupt, like, 'Wally, I am working on developing and strengthening myself as a leader and preparing myself for a future role in this company. I am looking for honest input, and I would appreciate getting your take. I already know what you think of my technical skills. I got that from my performance review. But I would like more clarity about some specific leadership areas. I wonder if I could have some time to discuss those with you . . .' How does that sound?"

"Wow, Cynthia, you make it sound so easy."

"You need to put it in your own words, of course. But something like that. That way, you're not barging in on him; you're asking for some time he can plan and giving him time to think about his response. I am pretty sure he will respond positively to that kind of request."

"Am I supposed to do that for real?" He could feel his heart pounding at the thought.

"Yes," she said, looking at her calendar. "I'm thinking that before we meet again in two weeks would be ideal. So we can talk about what you heard from him. Can you make that happen?"

Rafa was squirming in his seat. He spoke in a rush. "Sure, I'll try. I'll ask him. Hopefully, he has the time. I'll guarantee you that I will ask. It will be uncomfortable and I will be uncomfortable, but I will ask him."

"Good. And it's not a bad thing to feel uncomfortable. That means it's pushing your envelope—a real learning opportunity. So that is good news. And, one more thing, Rafa. You know what? I am going to send you an instrument that may help you gather feedback from other people, including Wally." Cynthia jotted down a note to remind herself. "Have you ever heard of the Johari Window?"

Rafa shook his head.

"Well, it's been around for sixty years or so. It's a very informative and easy-to-use framework for getting an idea of how you see yourself vis-à-vis others, and how they see you in ways that you're not aware of. It's really interesting. I will email it to you later today, and I'll include a description about how to use it. Basically, here's what you will be looking at." She started making a rough drawing on her notepad.

"Picture four boxes that are like four rooms. Room 1 is the part of ourselves that we see and others see. That's the public arena. Room 2 is what others see or know about us, but that we are unaware of. These are our blind spots. Room 3 is the unconscious or subconscious part of us that no one sees, not us or others. And Room 4 is our private space, what we know about ourselves but keep from others. That is our hidden space. There is actually a set of adjectives you can have people respond to. You'll see what I mean."

"How is that different from a 360?" Rafa asked, glancing at his watch.

"Well," Cynthia replied, "just a quick example, I promise. I never would have used the word 'caring' to describe myself, but that adjective came up a lot from others about me. On the other hand, they also said 'tense,' a word I also never would have applied to myself. It forced me to look at what I was doing, and how I was reacting in front of others."

"So what do you want me to do with the windows? Do you want me to give it to Wally to fill out?"

"Well, you could give him the list of adjectives and see which ones he thinks apply to you, or ask Wally some questions based on the adjectives that will draw out feedback you can use. But I think it might be useful for you to apply it to yourself. Take a look at it when I send it and see what you think. I would like to see you at least complete it for yourself. OK? And why don't I complete one for you too? We can compare notes next time we meet."

Rafa tapped out "Johari window" and looked up from his tablet, clearly spent.

"Had enough?"

Rafa stood up. "More than. I have a bunch of goals to rewrite and focus on. This Johari thing. And an interview with Wally. And my work. I think that's plenty."

"It is. But you have a whole two weeks. You can do it. And I am really looking forward to seeing your reworked goals and hearing about what you are doing as you work through them."

Rafa's eyes widened as he spoke. "A big agenda. So are we back to the Bean Counter's Café at 7 A.M., or do you want to move the time and place again?"

"Well, that's up to you. The office was better for me today, but if you would prefer the café, that should be fine. Whatever you want works for me."

"You know, Cynthia, actually I am fine with here. I like your office." He turned and pointed to Camelback Mountain. "I love the view."

Cynthia looked out the window. "Hmmm. Me too. Very restorative. Maybe I should move my desk so I can see it more easily. I love the lighting this time of day. The glow. Nice, huh?"

"Very nice. The perks of leadership, right?" They both laughed, and Rafa said, "Okay, I'll see you in two weeks with homework in hand. All of it!"

Rafa checked his inbox Thursday morning and found what struck him as a curt email from Cynthia:

Just checking in to see how things are going with Wally.

I have attached the information about the Johari Window, as we discussed during our last meeting. Give it a look and try it out. Call me if you have any problems.

Regards,

Cynthia

It had been only two days since they met! Cynthia was already on his back about Wally. Didn't she trust him when he said he was going to make the call? And then there was the Johari Window thing, which he had absolutely no interest in doing. He didn't see the point of it. It seemed like more busy work. He had already completed a 360 and a performance review. How much more feedback did he need? Cynthia didn't seem to care that he had job responsibilities beyond doing her mentoring homework. At least she could have asked about his time constraints before she loaded on more assignments. A *simple, "Will this work for you, given your workload at the moment?" would have been nice. But no, she forgets that I have a real job besides mentoring.*

The more he thought about it, the more resentful he became. *Oh crap, there's an attachment. The adjective thing.* Well, it could wait—he had work to do.

Throughout the morning, as he worked on the financials for the coming quarter, the numbers didn't come together the way they usually did. His mentoring assignment was nagging at him, and he couldn't concentrate. By noon, his head was pounding. When Scott stopped by to ask if he wanted to get a sandwich, he begged off. "Too much work to do," he said. "Rain check?" He was in no mood to grab a bite with his coworkers, although it didn't escape his notice that Scott actually seemed disappointed.

Rafa decided to eat an energy bar at his desk and tighten up his goal. *At least I'll be doing something productive that actually might affect my career*, he thought. The pulsing subsided. He already felt calmer and less stressed.

Rafa took out his tablet and typed the word "listening." He stared at it for several minutes, hoping it would inspire him. How was he supposed to make listening SMART? It was irritating that Cynthia wouldn't accept "work on listening" as a goal. Writing was not his strong point. This just felt like another exercise in semantics.

"Listen to others," he typed. *Okay, now make it specific.* But nothing came to him. He reviewed his notes. *Oh, yeah, goals:* "Why is this goal important to your development?" He had to admit that some of the Cynthia's comments about listening had made good sense to him. He finished off the energy bar and washed it down with the cold coffee that was left in his cup. *Whatever.*

Okay, well, improving relationships with my coworkers is definitely on there. He started his list with that, and was surprised to find that once he started typing the ideas began to flow. Each idea generated another—"improving relationships with my coworkers, building consensus, getting buy-in on my ideas, getting others to listen to me, gauging where people are coming from." *Whoa. That was five.*

He started to work on turning his starter goal into a SMART goal: "Improve relationships, consensus, and buy-in with coworkers through active listening." Yes! He gathered steam as he wrote on. "During the next quarter, demonstrate listening by paraphrasing, making eye contact, agreeing, and acknowledging during all business conversations, meetings, and interactions with coworkers."

He sat back and looked at his list. *Excellent.*

He rummaged through his desk drawer, searching for a second energy bar before tackling his next goal. *Huh.* This goal seemed more complicated. He began with, "Don't push your ideas." That didn't really sound like much of a goal. He deleted that and started again. "Work on being more collaborative." He stared at that phrase for a while, but it didn't seem to take him in any direction. *How do you do that?* he wondered, as he finished off the second energy bar.

He looked at his watch. People would be coming back from lunch soon, and he needed to get back to those financials. Cynthia really didn't seem to understand the enormous amount of pressure he was under to get his work out. And that was ironic, given the little framed quote she had posted near her workstation: "Seek first to understand, then to be understood." Maybe she should look at that more often.

Oh, wait.

He looked at his goals and wrote, "Work to understand others' positions before pushing my own point of view." He laughed aloud as he quickly deleted the last six words. That would not go over well with Cynthia. "before asserting my own point of view." *No . . .* "before explaining my own position." *No.* Maybe "Work to understand others' positions" was enough? It would have to be.

Rafa walked down the hall to the break room and got a soda to wash down the energy bars. He felt the sugar and caffeine surge through his body and hit his brain. He needed to make that goal SMART for Cynthia, and then he could get back to his real work. *Focus.*

He walked back to his desk, opened his tablet, and started typing. "Create a climate of teamwork and collaboration during all team problem solving sessions by exploring and understanding others' positions first before stating my own views . . ." *Whoa, where did that come from?* He was on a roll. He decided to add a third goal, addressing the creation of a new department. Why not? It was a good idea. Cynthia had even said that herself. And someone had to get the wheels in motion.

Rafa felt pretty pleased with himself. He had a reasonable draft for Cynthia to review. The office activity was building up again as his coworkers wandered in from lunch. He looked at his watch.

He was exhausted and jumpy, and he still had to get through the rest of the afternoon. But he'd done good work on his mentoring assignment. Cynthia couldn't say he hadn't. He took out his phone and texted her:

> Tired and hungry. Finally wrote some SMART goals. Felt like English 101. Hope I passed the course! :-)

He pressed Send with a vengeance, and immediately regretted it. Was that too snarky? *Oh well. At least she'll know I'm trying.* He shrugged it off, eager to get back to his real work.

A wrapped sandwich landed on his desk. He looked up to see Scott smiling at him. "Dude, I know you didn't eat any real food, and that's bad for all of us. Consider this a gift for the protection of your coworkers!" He walked off to his own cubicle.

As Rafa devoured the sandwich, he thought hard about assumptions.

———————

Cynthia found texting annoying except when she really needed to contact someone in a hurry and had no time to chat on the phone. When Rafa's text arrived, she had to think for a moment to realize what that ringtone signified. *Why is he texting me? We don't have a meeting today.* Then she read it, and reread it.

"He's whining to me! In a text!" she exclaimed aloud. She shook her head. *He sounds like my kids when they were young:* "Mom, are we there yet?" English 101! Happy face. He had clearly done the work against his will—for her, not for himself. *Grow up, Rafa.*

The more she thought about it, the more annoyed she became. His pointless oppositional attitude irritated her. She started to text a reply, but caught herself. She was doing exactly what Rafa was doing—reacting. She was supposed to be the mentor. *He's young, and this text message only confirms it.*

She made a note to bring it up at their next meeting. Then she glanced at the clock. *Ah, he worked over lunch. He's hungry and tired, and he's grumpy about it.* She had learned long ago that some people get irritable and impulsive when they are hungry, which was why she never scheduled policy or strategy sessions right before lunch.

She visualized Rafa hunched over his desk, trying to plow through this assignment instead of eating. *But he did it, to his credit. That's something. And if he didn't see the value of the SMART goal work, well, maybe that's on me. I have to take some ownership there.* Her annoyance at Rafa shifted to regret about her own contribution. She should have made sure he was on board, or OK with it, or understood it. Lesson learned.

She decided to reply to his text after all:

> Rafa. Sorry that the goal setting and SMART goals assignment was such a challenge. I see now that I should have spent more time helping you understand the how and why of it all. That's on me. I owe you a real lunch. Cynthia.

Rafa tossed the sandwich wrapper into his wastebasket. He felt much more ready to tackle his work, and much more regretful for sending that text to Cynthia. So when he saw her quick response—she'd let him off the hook!—he breathed a sign of relief. Maybe all that work on goals had been worth the effort. And he was getting lunch out of the deal! He made a note to himself to remember to eat a real lunch more often. Scott had a point; it did seem to improve his mood. Was he that scary?

Rafa's smartphone beeped at him, displaying the calendar alarm he'd set: REQUEST APPT W/WALLY. He shook his head. *Guess I've put it off as long as I can.* He was annoyed at himself for finding this so difficult. *Suck it up and just do it,* he said to himself. He had to at least try to connect. If Wally had no time, well, that wasn't his fault. He would have made the effort to ask, anyway.

He started to compose an email but drew a blank after typing "Wally"—what had Cynthia suggested? He looked at his notes and used some of the language she'd offered:

> Wally,
>
> I am working on my leadership development with my mentor, Cynthia Colson, and she suggested that I get your perspective on areas for personal growth, beyond my technical skills. I wonder if you would have some time in the next few days to discuss these issues.
>
> Thanks,
> Rafa

That seemed pretty neutral. Rafa was secretly hoping his email would fall through the cracks, or that Wally would take his usual week or so to reply. But later that very same day, Wally sent him an Outlook appointment: an hour with Wally—tomorrow afternoon!

Digging Deeper

Questions for Mentors:

1. After two months, what did Rafa say he was getting from his mentoring relationship?

2. What value would your mentees say they get from your mentoring relationship?

3. How is mentoring providing value to you? What can you do to increase its value to both you and your mentee?

4. What did Cynthia do or say that pushed Rafa out of his comfort zone?

5. How frequently do your mentees get out of their comfort zone on their own? What do you do to push your mentees out of their comfort zone?

6. What more can you do to help your mentees feel more comfortable about taking risks?

7. How do you know when to push your mentee and when to hold back?

Questions for Mentees:

1. What value was Rafa receiving from his mentoring experience up to this point?

2. How is mentoring providing value for you right now? How might you add value to your relationship?

3. What value do you think your mentor might be getting from your mentoring relationship? What questions might you ask to find out for sure?

4. What were some ways that Cynthia pushed Rafa out of his comfort zone?

5. In what ways has your mentor pushed you out of your comfort zone? Do you think your mentor could do more in this area, or less?

6. What more can your mentor do to help you feel more comfortable taking risks? What's the best way to let your mentor know what you need?

7. How do you know when to speak up and when to hold back in talking with your mentor?

The Fifth Meeting: Straight Talk

One week later Rafa arrived at Cynthia's office promptly at 3 P.M. with two large lattes in hand, a peace offering. Cynthia's face lit up when she saw the coffee. "Good timing," she said. "I mean the coffee. It's just what I needed."

Rafa sat in his usual seat and powered up his tablet.

"Thanks for sending your goals so I could review them before the meeting," Cynthia said, reaching for a chocolate to go with her latte. "That will help us to get the most out of this hour."

"Sure, no problem. Did you get a chance to look at my agenda for today?"

"I did. And I'm glad you started to put in the 'Catching Up' as a formal item. I think it's important, especially for this meeting. There are some things we definitely need to catch up on."

"OK, do you want to go first?" Rafa asked.

"I do have a couple of things, but why don't you start with the Roundtable. I am curious—how did it go?"

"Well, it was really interesting. I think we were all anxious to hear about where everyone was, and how they were using mentoring and what they were working on. So they asked each of us to go around and give a quick status update—you know, on how often we were meeting, what we were talking about, and goals we were focusing on, if any." Rafa smiled. "You would have been very proud of us. Compared to everyone else, we are way ahead of the game."

Cynthia looked surprised. "Really? How so?"

"Well, at least half the group has met only once or twice with their mentor. And there doesn't seem to be much focus or structure in place. At least two people said they felt like they were imposing on their mentor's time. So even when they had something to run by their mentor, they didn't do it. And one of them is getting flack from her manager because he seems paranoid about her meeting with a mentor. I felt bad for her. I certainly don't have that issue with Wally."

Rafa leaned forward, his expression earnest. "Now I can see why, early on, you were pushing me to nail down some agreements about how we would meet. I can see that it really makes a difference. You know, I think that I might be the only one in the group who has any specific written goals and is actually working on them. Kind of felt good." He smiled, and Cynthia smiled back.

"Well," she said, "I'm glad for us, but disappointed for everyone else." She took a moment to make a note to herself to call the program director and see what was going on there. Maybe there was something she could do to help get the program in gear.

"But I do think the Roundtable had some real value," Rafa continued. "For one thing, I saw a lot of note-taking going on when I described our process. I think it opened a lot of eyes. And one of my friends texted me right after and asked if we could go for coffee because he had some questions about what we were doing. It will be interesting to see what he wants."

Cynthia agreed. "Yes. I am very interested to see where this goes with the rest of the group. Keep me updated, if you will."

Rafa nodded. "Definitely." He paused. "So, now what?"

"I want to talk about two things," Cynthia began. "Your text to me last week and the goal-setting work you did." She took out her smartphone and read Rafa's text back to him: "Tired and hungry. Finally wrote some SMART goals. Felt like English 101. Hope I passed the course! Smiley face." Cynthia looked up at him but didn't say another word.

"Sounds pretty lame," Rafa confessed. "I'm sorry. I felt bad about it the second I pressed Send. I sound like a whiner."

"You were whining, weren't you? But the issue I want to talk to you about is less about that and more about the danger of emailing, texting, or communicating to someone when you're feeling angry, irritable, or grouchy. Was that a wise thing to do?"

"No, I guess not. Probably not too smart."

"I don't think so either. And it's the kind of thing that can really get you in trouble in business. Just remember, whoever sees it can forward it—you never know where it might end up and who might read it. If you're angry or grousing about something, that's the permanent impression that will stay with someone."

"Good reminder."

"But I am not saying don't do or say anything when you have an issue. It doesn't mean stay silent. Any ideas about what you might do differently next time you're feeling like that?"

"Well, I won't be texting, that's for sure. If I am upset about something, well, I guess I should write an email and ask for help or clarification or something like that. Or write the email and 'Save as draft' and see how I feel about the whole thing later. Is that better?"

"Much better. Good for you. Enough said on that topic. However, you did communicate something that was very important for me to hear. Your tone told me that you didn't like doing the work and you were struggling with it. The 'English 101 assignment' comment? That told me you didn't fully understand the value of doing it. It was my fault."

"How in the world was that your fault?"

"It made me realize that when I give work to anyone, like one of my own direct reports, I need to make sure they understand the context, importance, and value of the assignment I've delegated to them. I would never want anyone to think that I'm just assigning busy work. Of course, I would hope they would give me the benefit of the doubt."

"I think I was just venting from the frustration of wordsmithing my SMART goals. It just doesn't come easy to me."

"No, I do know that, and I should have offered my support earlier along the way. I should have helped you get started and given you an opportunity to ask me questions so that you were clear about what you needed to do. And I should have antici- pated a little of this. Most people struggle with formulating goals. I have trouble doing it myself, and I have my people developing goals all the time. Anyway, and not to belabor the point, I apol- ogize for not providing enough backup for you so that you felt comfortable."

"Well, thanks. I appreciate that. But no worries, Cynthia; eventually I worked through it. I had to constantly revisit your question—*Why? Why is this important to me and my development as a leader?* That actually stirred the pot."

"So, how about if we start by reviewing the goals first? And then, creating a game plan for implementation and trying to find some ways of measuring progress? It can be a tricky business, but we need to do it."

"Sounds great," said Rafa.

———

Cynthia looked over Rafa's list of goals.

"I see that you're still persisting with this business reorg goal. Rafa, let's put that one on the back burner. I'd like to start with the first two and then let's see where things go. OK?"

"Sure," he said.

Did he look disappointed? Annoyed? Cynthia studied Rafa but couldn't get a read on where his head was just at that moment. "Before we dig in, are there any other things we want to catch up on? Do you have any other issues?"

Rafa looked down, avoiding eye contact. "There is one other thing," he said in a flat tone. "I debated mentioning it, but you said early on to be real, not to hold back. So, yes, I was run- ning on empty when I wrote that text, but one of the reasons I think I was so irritated was actually because of the email you sent that morning. It was kind of abrupt, and you asked if I had made contact with Wally—just two days after our last meeting.

To be perfectly honest, I felt like you were micromanaging me. Like you didn't trust that I would get to it on my own."

Cynthia looked blank for a second. That was not what she'd meant to communicate at all. It had just been a busy morning and she'd wanted to get that note out. She should take her own advice. "You're completely right," she said, shaking her head. "I shouldn't have written that. I was in a rush, and being superefficient to a fault. I needed to trust that since you said you would do it, you would. I'm really sorry. I guess we both need to work on our written communication skills."

Rafa exhaled audibly, and his shoulders relaxed. He smiled. "Thanks. I'm glad I got that off my chest."

"I'm glad you did too. I know that sometimes it is difficult to say what you are really feeling in front of me. I appreciate that you took the risk in being so frank. And I hope you will continue with that kind of honesty—better to get it all out there than have resentments build up."

She looked down at the agenda. "OK. Shall we talk about the Wally meeting? I appreciated your note letting me know you two had met."

"We did indeed," said Rafa, and launched into his story with enthusiasm. "So. After whining to myself about how could I possibly write the email to Wally"—he smiled—"I did it using pretty much the language you had suggested. I also mentioned that you were my mentor, and that you had suggested that it might be a good idea to get his perspective, which made me feel less like I was begging and more like this was a legitimate thing to do."

"That's reasonable, and it's true," said Cynthia. She was pleased that he had been able to get out of his snit and pull himself together so quickly. Rafa seemed to be very good at course correcting.

"Well. Honestly, I was hoping that Wally would forget to answer or put it off for a week, but he actually set an appointment almost immediately—for the next day. Which freaked me out, because I didn't have time to prepare for it. On the other hand,

I didn't have time to overthink it, either. But I have to admit, I was nervous."

He was into the story now, barely stopping for breath. "Anyway, I showed up, and Wally actually seemed very pleased that I had asked for the meeting. I remembered you mentioned that you like it when your people ask you for feedback because it made it easier to give it and they were more receptive. Basically, Wally said the same thing, which was a huge relief.

"He said that he was glad to hear that I was working on developing my leadership skills with a mentor. And he actually said he had noticed some improvement in my relationship with the team. He was also very complimentary about the presentation and how I handled it."

"Terrific," said Cynthia. "What was his perspective on the issue with your team and that early dissension? Was he aware of it?"

"He did comment on it, which was interesting, because he didn't seem to be paying much attention to that stuff. In fact, I always thought he left the team alone and it was off his radar. So I didn't know if he knew we were struggling. But he did. He said that several of my coworkers had come to him complaining about the trouble I was having with the team's recommendations. They felt like I was bullying them into changing their position—and apparently this wasn't the first time they'd expressed having difficulty with me and my style." Rafa stopped.

"That must have been hard to hear," said Cynthia.

"Yeah. I was surprised, and it just felt bad to hear. Who knew?"

Cynthia considered mentioning that Rafa should have known just from reading his 360, but she thought better of it, and Rafa was still talking.

"From early on, it turns out, some of them were having a hard time with me. I asked Wally why he hadn't said anything to me about it, or done anything."

"Good question to ask." *Hmm*—Wally was a lot more hands-off than she was.

"Wally's view was that if the issue was that important to them, they needed to address it with me directly and that he wasn't going to intercede. He told them that he expected them to have the maturity to be able to talk to me about it. Well, none of them did." He rolled his eyes. "Would have been good to know."

"What do you think you would have done with that information?" Cynthia asked.

"I don't know. Probably discounted it," said Rafa. Cynthia noted that his self-awareness had risen several levels in the last two-and-a-half months.

"Anyway, I asked him why it hadn't come up in my performance review, and he said that he didn't want to 'burst my bubble'—his words, not mine. He thought that I was a little too aggressive and cocky, yes, but that my coworkers also needed to raise their level of assertiveness. Believe it or not, he said he would rather have employees like me who fight for their ideas and believe in what they are doing than people who just show up and do their job and don't rock the boat. He actually complimented me on my spirit. That really was a surprise."

"That's nice feedback. Were you pleased?"

"Well, surprised. And yes, pleased. But don't get too excited yet, because he gave me some other feedback too. He felt that I did need to learn how to play well with others—you know, deal more effectively with coworkers. So even though he liked my spirit and all that stuff, he was disappointed that I wasn't using my influence to my advantage. It seems that I was turning coworkers off to my ideas, not turning them on. And here's the big shocker: he had apparently told the people who recruited me in the first place that he was looking for someone who had spirit—a go-getter; someone he could rely on to motivate the rest of the team."

Rafa shook his head. "Cynthia," he said, looking her in the eye, "I had no idea about that. I thought he resented me because he hadn't been the one to hire me directly. But I guess maybe I just misinterpreted a few things . . . You know, his comments actually hit home for me. He made a really valid point. I have been thinking a lot about what he said."

Cynthia leaned forward. "So what was the learning point for you from that comment?"

"Well, this leadership thing. I am trying to get ahead, and I want my career to move forward, now! All this time, I've been thinking about it in terms of a job and a position. But when Wally said that I wasn't as big an influence as he had hoped I would be, that kind of hit me in the gut. And it reminded me—" Rafa stopped for a moment.

"Pardon me for bringing this up," he said, "but it reminded me of when I was captain of my prep school team. We were pretty decent and could have gone all the way to the playoffs, but we had a couple of guys on the team who were talented enough but just wouldn't do the work. I was the captain. It was my job to lead. But I couldn't get the guys to stretch properly, eat well, or practice more. One guy ended up pulling a groin muscle, and another one got into a slump and wouldn't take extra batting practice. And another guy ran out of gas in the late innings.

"At the time, I blamed those guys for not bringing their best and giving 100 percent, and that's still valid. But now I see that I had a part in it too. I couldn't influence them to do anything different. Maybe if I had had a better handle on how to motivate and influence them we could have been a better team. I hadn't fully understood that until Wally said what he said."

Cynthia sat back in her chair and smiled, reflecting on how gratifying it was to see the growth in Rafa's self-awareness. Most people Cynthia knew got the "blame others" part, but they rarely saw their personal role in contributing to the problem. As Rafa continued, she brought her chair closer, eager to hear more.

"Cynthia, I can see now that I need to learn how to become a more positive influence. I think when I can get my coworkers to believe in an idea, and we all get behind it, then there's energy and commitment for the task. And that's what Wally told me is lacking from the team. In fact, he told me that until recently, the team's lack of productivity was partly because they were spending too much time and energy fending off my ideas. They had no more stomach for developing new ideas of their own, and they just stalled out."

Rafa shook his head and lowered his voice. "That was not fun to hear. He was basically saying that I was making things worse even though my intentions were good. Still, at least he did get my intention. He knows that I'm committed to improving our processes and streamlining our system. It was just that he wasn't prepared to invest in my ideas or back me until I had earned the support of the others. He was waiting for me to figure that out. Who knew?"

"That's quite some feedback," said Cynthia. "It's interesting that he told you he had already seen a change in you."

"Yeah, that was good to hear. And you'll be happy to know that he was really glad you were my mentor. He was pretty confident that you would be able to help me get some insight into all of this and turn myself around. He has a lot of faith in your abilities, by the way." Rafa tented his forefingers and slowly pointed them directly at her.

"That's always nice to hear."

"Yeah, he said that he'd decided to be hands-off with me about my interaction with the team because he felt like I had to come to it on my own. Or maybe he just thought I wouldn't take it the right way. He had hoped that NextGen would help, but thought it focused too much on leadership principles. That's why he was such a big proponent of the mentoring. He wanted someone to help me examine what I was doing and explore what was working and what more I needed to bring to the table. All this time, I had been wondering why he hadn't talked to me or given me feedback or something. I just figured he didn't like me. Turns out it was his management style. So this was a big deal for me."

"Sounds like it was. So what are you going to do with that? Does it influence any of the goals you've already set?"

"No—in fact, I think it just reinforces the two goals that I put down, the listening and the 'seek first to understand' goal. At least those are good places to start. Plus, as Wally pointed out, he has seen some change in me over the last month, especially in preparation for that big presentation. He was totally aware of the friction between the group and me in terms of the recommendation. He told me he was actually planning to intervene and mandate a solution, but then I came back to the team and offered a new approach for bringing us together. It was a very satisfying moment for him. That was really nice to hear too."

"I'll bet. So, anything else you and Wally discussed that you want to talk about?"

"Well, for one thing, he offered to meet with me on a regular basis, like monthly, to talk about how things are going with the team. You know, my relationship with them, influencing them, the leadership side. And he said definitely to come to him with any problems I am having or if I feel stuck. A nice offer."

Cynthia removed her glasses. "Rafa, is this the same Wally you have complained about who doesn't provide opportunity, is behind the times, and doesn't let you engage and participate with problem solving? Doesn't sound like the same guy to me."

"I know." Rafa uncrossed his legs, stood up for a moment, and waved his hands around. "Who is this guy, right?" He laughed.

Sitting back down, he continued, "And when he offered his help, I did say to him that I hoped the team would get a better crack at being involved in problem solving, and he challenged me back. He said that he hadn't involved the team because there was inconsistency in the energy and commitment to participate. For example, he didn't want someone like me to go out into the business units and prove to be a valuable resource and then prompt other business units to demand the same level of service. He knew most of his other FAs wouldn't be able to provide those services. He challenged me to motivate the team, to get them engaged so that everyone is prepared to provide consultation services to our business units by the first quarter of next year. That's pretty exciting. Don't you think?"

"That's great. And you get to lead the effort."

"I do and I will. And it will be a welcome challenge. Boy, I have wanted us to do this for some time. I had no idea what was holding Wally back from letting us do it. I never guessed his reasoning. I just assumed he didn't think we could do it or he wanted the responsibility for himself."

"So that's perhaps a good thing to remember, moving forward." Cynthia offered.

"Yeah, definitely. I have been complaining about Wally and my position and lack of opportunity—and here I had it, and him, figured out all wrong—totally."

"Rafa," Cynthia continued, "remember when I suggested you sit down with Wally and get some feedback?"

Rafa nodded.

"How did you feel at the time about doing that, during our meeting?"

"How did I feel? I dreaded it. I resented it. I was nervous. I came to it thinking, 'Why do I want to sit down with someone I don't relate to, who doesn't like me, doesn't get me?' What's the value in that? What is he going to say that is going to have any use for me? That's what I was thinking."

"And think about how much you learned as a result. So what's the lesson in all of that for you?"

"Well, number one, again, don't make assumptions about people's thinking or motives. That's for sure. Early on I think I got a certain impression of Wally as a leader, and after that everything he did just reinforced my original viewpoint. I wish I had known what he was really thinking. So, two, I should ask direct questions to get clarity or confirmation and real answers. That's a big lesson also. And there's another leadership issue in there for me . . ." Rafa paused.

"Which is . . .?"

"It's that I don't really agree with Wally's strategy. I think he was off course on this one." He looked at Cynthia to see her reaction.

"What do you mean, 'off course'?"

"Well, do you think he should have kept quiet? After all, he has a team he thinks is underperforming. He lowers the standard by not demanding anything from them because he doesn't think he can get them to do what needs to be done. Instead, he sort of implied that he hired some kind of upstart rookie to come in and shake things up. He hoped the rookie, namely me, would make happen what he hasn't been able to do. I mean, Cynthia, does that seem fair? Is that good leadership? Would you do it that way? This is an honest question—what do you think?"

Cynthia hesitated, struggling to find the right reply before she spoke up. His question required tactful, skillful navigation. She was searching for the balance between being honest and authentic with her mentee, and not criticizing a colleague. "This is where our confidentiality agreement works two ways, Rafa. Right? You know that discussing colleagues is a sensitive area."

"Yes, I do know that," said Rafa. "But this is an important issue for me."

"Right. Well, I have to say that would not have been my approach. It isn't my style. And no, I don't think it was fair to put the burden on you to shake up your team. I do see where he was coming from. He has a fairly entrenched, veteran group who have been resistant to change. And it's a family company with values that reward loyalty, so I'm sure he knew that he wasn't going to be able to move anyone out.

"Nevertheless," she continued cautiously, "a new, young employee shouldn't be expected to take on that assignment, and certainly not without knowing that is his assignment and that he has the support of his senior leader."

Rafa released a deep sigh. "Thank you. I feel better already. It has been a harder year than I think it needed to be because of his approach."

"So even though you now know what his intentions were, you are still tasked with the same assignment. And it's a tough task: you have to motivate your team to get out of their comfort zone, learn some new skills, and perform in a new way. And you have a deadline. But at least you know you have Wally's support."

As Cynthia summarized his position, Rafa tried to take it all in. "It *is* going to be a tough one. I have to think on it. The timing is perfect though, since you and I are working on goals. I know just where to apply them. I have my own little laboratory to experiment in."

"That's true. And now we have a perfect way of measuring your success at listening, building collaboration, and creating buy-in. The ultimate test of success is going to be measured by whether or not your team is ready to assume the new consulting role Wally has in mind for them next year."

"So that's a good place to start," said Rafa. "How do I begin? It's kind of overwhelming. Plus, I don't want to lose momentum by doing something stupid." He looked at Cynthia. Maybe she'd actually help him out this time and not make him do all the work.

But she was scrolling through her contact list.

Finally she looked up. "Rafa, I have a couple of thoughts and a learning opportunity that might help as you face this." She wrote a name and contact information on a sticky note and handed it to him. "I want you to meet my friend Tom Seligman."

"Should I know that name?"

"I don't think so. He's COO of Boxworth Industries, and he implemented a huge change initiative with his sales and engineering teams just a couple of months ago. I don't know the details, but basically, his sales team was going out and making promises that his engineers had to deliver on without really understanding what they had committed to do. Also, his sales folks, who just wanted to close deals, often promised things that couldn't be delivered. So Tom set a new model in motion where sales and engineering teamed together to make the sales call, commitments, deliverables, and the whole ball of wax. Both groups had to move out of their comfort zone. He got two very disparate groups to come together. He got their buy-in and got them prepared to speak each other's language. I think his story would teach you a lot."

"Sounds really interesting," said Rafa. He could feel his excitement building. *This seems like a big deal.* "Do you really think he would meet with me?"

Cynthia raised her eyebrows. "I do. He owes me a favor, and he's a great guy. I'll give him a heads-up call and make sure he's got the time, and then I will send you both an email introduction, then you guys can take it from there. I am eager to hear what you learn from him. But—don't meet with him unless you go in fully prepared. Know what you are looking for and the questions you want to ask him. He is a very busy guy."

"I will," Rafa promised, as he finished typing his notes. "Don't worry."

"I won't. I am really pleased for you, Rafa. And I am proud of you. You are a talented young guy. You want to learn, and I like that. You are open to the feedback you get—the good, the bad, and the ugly. I like that you take the positive feedback in stride. You don't let it go to your head. And you also don't let negative and challenging feedback weigh you down. You take it in and manage to stay open. And you do something with it. It's the right approach. I like that. And you are putting your energy in the right place. It's all good."

Rafa blushed. "Thanks for saying that. I actually was wondering if I had blown it with you over that text. I appreciate the confidence you have in me."

Cynthia shrugged. "Mistakes happen. Judgments can be wrong. You're still learning. I just want you to keep learning from your mistakes. We all have made them. But we learn. I learned, and you are learning."

Rafa was quiet for a moment, looking at the afternoon sun hitting Camelback Mountain. "OK," he said, "so this isn't exactly a mistake, but I do want to confess that I didn't get to the Johari Window stuff yet. I looked at it, but I really haven't had time to take it on. Shall I start that up next week?"

"You know, I think we can revisit that some other time. At this point for you, with the feedback you have received, maybe it won't be that useful right now." She could see the relief on Rafa's face. "And I can see you weren't that thrilled to do it."

"It's true, I confess. I just didn't want to be that obvious."

"I'll make a deal with you, though. Let's set aside the Johari Window, and instead, since Wally has laid out a rather commanding challenge with your team, I want to suggest a book for you to read."

Rafa couldn't hide his disappointment with being given another assignment—this time reading.

Cynthia caught his reaction and responded immediately. "Don't panic! You'll like it, I promise. It's a book by Patrick Lencioni called *The Five Dysfunctions of a Team*, and it is right up your alley. You're going to have to work with your team, and if they're not on board, you'll have to figure out why. And FYI, I usually find that when teams are underperforming, or resisting, it rarely has anything to do with a lack of skill sets."

"What *does* it have to do with?"

Cynthia smiled. "Oh, no. You're not going to get the answer from me on this one. You're going to find it yourself in *The Five Dysfunctions*. That I guarantee. It is short, very readable, and you can knock it off this weekend for sure."

"I'm on it," he said, making a note to download it as soon as he got back to his office. "That, by the way, may be a first for me. I don't love reading."

"I can see that—you're an action-oriented guy. That's why this book is perfect for you—it's relevant to your problem and can solve a lot of mysteries for you. Which I guess I made clear—and good for me on that one—because I can see that you're not secretly pouting about having to do a book report. And I know that if I hadn't clarified it, you would have spoken up and challenged me on it."

"I would have, you're right."

"You need to take charge of your own energy and enthusiasm for a project or assignment, whatever it is."

Rafa held up his hands in mock surrender. "OK, OK, point taken. You're right. That is on me to do that, because when I don't see the application or practicality of it, I do see it as busy work."

Cynthia looked at her watch. "Oops, I've got more meetings this afternoon, believe it or not." She stood up and straightened her skirt, and Rafa closed up his tablet and stood as well.

"OK," she said, "lots to think about and plan for. Thanks for the coffee, Rafa. I will send you an email introducing you to Tom. Look for that coming your way. Next time we meet, I want to hear about your conversation—and your impressions about the book. I am sure you will get some great insights from both."

"I'm sure I will. And thanks for everything, especially the introduction to Tom. Oh—and don't forget that lunch you promised me!"

Cynthia watched as Rafa strolled out of the room and down the hall, tossing his empty cup in the trash. *He's already carrying himself with more confidence.*

———————

Rafa left Cynthia's office and rode the elevator down to his floor, in a hurry to order the Lencioni book and contact Tom Seligman. Once again, Cynthia had challenged him to find answers for himself. Rather than telling him what she thought, she had gently drawn him into conversation. But instead of resenting it, he was beginning to appreciate the genius of it. *A good technique. Maybe I should try it out with our team.*

He sat down at his desk and drew a big red question mark on a sticky note as a reminder to ask questions. He stuck it on his monitor where he'd be sure to see it. Then he googled "Tom Seligman" and "Boxworth Industries."

This guy was a heavyweight. The opportunity for a sit-down with such a high-profile leader was indeed rare, especially for someone in his position.

Rafa sat back in his chair, stretched his arms backward as far as he could reach, and whooped. "Allllllllllright, Cynthia!" He laughed when his coworker popped his head up over the cubicle partition to see what all the excitement was about.

The next morning, Rafa found two emails from Cynthia waiting in his inbox. One contained Tom Siegman's contact information. The second was addressed to both Rafa and Tom.

> With this email, I am introducing you to each other.
>
> Tom, Rafa is the financial analyst I mentioned to you yesterday. Like you, he isn't afraid to change things up. However, Rafa's situation is somewhat different in three respects: (1) he is young, (2) he's not in charge, and (3) he is also dealing with a culture that is resistant to change. I know you will be able to provide some excellent insight and support for him. I am sure you will both enjoy meeting each other.
>
> Best,
> Cynthia

Rafa winced when he read the word "young" in Cynthia's email, but he let it go. It was a small irritation, and Cynthia was awesome. He liked her direct-to-the-point, yet easygoing style.

Rafa spent the weekend reading *The Five Dysfunctions* and taking copious notes. Cynthia was right. It didn't take long to read, and he couldn't get enough of it. The fictional team Lencioni created could have been Wally's team, dysfunctions and all! Rafa was beginning to see that all teams might have similar problems, and that he didn't have to figure everything out by himself. During the week, he read the book a second time, this time focusing on how the model applied to him and his colleagues.

As he reread his notes, an Outlook alert drew his attention. He smiled as he saw Cynthia's email appear on his screen with the subject line "Next Meeting." Rafa had been thinking about what he wanted to put on the agenda for their next meeting and was glad to see that he and Cynthia were in sync.

> Rafa,
>
> I owe you lunch! How about meeting at Nikki's? Given how much we have to discuss, let's block off a couple of hours. Would you mind if we moved our meeting to next Friday? That is the only day when I have a two-hour block of time available.
>
> I know you will want to talk about the Five Dysfunctions, and I am eager to hear what you are learning from reading it. We will probably want to talk about your meeting with Tom and how you are preparing for it, where you are with your personal development goals, and how you are doing with the team goal that Wally set for you.
>
> Since this is the three-month milestone in our mentoring relationship, let's save time at the end of the meeting to check in and see where we are at. We can talk about what is working and what is not, what we can do to improve our meetings and relationship, whether our process is holding up, and our satisfaction with progress on your leadership development.
>
> Please let me know if I am on track with these suggestions. I know you are working on an agenda.
>
> Cynthia

Ninety days! Unreal. Rafa couldn't believe how quickly three months had passed, and how his thinking had changed in such a short period of time.

He reread the email again to help him with his agenda. What did she mean by what is working and what is not? He shook it off and thought about the game he was going to on the weekend. He and Cynthia had started back in January, and now spring training was in its final month.

Digging Deeper

Questions for Mentors:

1. Most managers are given departmental goals, and direct reports usually complete some sort of personal development plan. Given the familiarity with goal execution, why is goal setting such a difficult task?

2. What is the value of having written goals?

3. Cynthia adopted the familiar SMART model for goal setting. What goal-setting models are you familiar with? How proficient are you at using them?

4. What is the advantage of applying a model to the goal-setting process?

5. Not every mentee is able to identify appropriate developmental goals important for his professional growth. Why is it so challenging for some mentees?

6. What challenges are you facing or have you faced in helping your mentees identify goals?

7. How would you describe the quality of the goals you and your mentee have set?

Questions for Mentees:

1. Rafa struggled with writing his goals. What do you think was getting in his way? What is the value of having written goals?

2. Many mentors and mentees find goal setting to be a difficult task. How challenging is it for you? Why?

3. Cynthia adopted the familiar SMART model for goal setting. What goal-setting models are you familiar with?

4. What is the advantage of using a model to set goals? Are you using a model to formulate your own goals?

5. Not every mentee is able to identify appropriate developmental goals that are important for their professional growth. What goals are you working on currently?

6. Why are the goals you identified important to your future development?

The Sixth Meeting: Holding Up a Mirror

Friday couldn't come fast enough for Rafa. And when it did, it was a perfect day, the kind of spring day that March visitors to Arizona dream about—warm but not hot, breezy but not windy, clear and not smoggy.

Rafa arrived at Nikki's early enough to ensure that he would be there on time and find a parking space in the lot. He turned off the engine and sat still, gathering his thoughts. He had been looking forward to this meeting; he had a lot of good stuff to talk about. But he was anxious about the check-in item Cynthia had mentioned in her latest email—he just couldn't let it go. *What's working and what isn't* . . .

His mind was spinning. *Is she having a problem with me that I don't know about? Did I do something wrong or disappoint her in some way?* He couldn't imagine what he might have done to upset her, but . . . As he walked toward the restaurant in search of his mentor, he knew he would find out soon enough.

———

Rafa and Cynthia arrived at the beautiful, ornately carved doorway of Nikki's at the same moment. As they went in and were shown to their table, they chatted about weekend plans—Rafa was going to a Cactus League game with a buddy, and Cynthia and her husband were going to a play. The waiter left them with menus to peruse, and they quickly made their choices.

Once the lunch order was under way, Rafa took out the agenda. It included all the items Cynthia had proposed in her email. He reeled off the items one by one and then paused. "I know check-in is scheduled for the end of our meeting, but it's been bugging me. I'm going to just ask about this straight out: Is there something wrong that I need to know about? Because if there is, I would rather discuss it up front, if that's alright with you."

Why is he looking so serious? "Rafa, what would give you the idea that something is wrong?"

"This check-in—'what's working and what isn't'? I assumed that was your subtle way of saying you want to talk about something wrong."

"Wow. Not at all!" *You just never know what's was going to push someone's buttons. I need to pay attention to that.* "I guess this is something new for you. Let me reassure you, there is nothing wrong. You should know by now that if I did have an issue, I wouldn't be subtle about it. "

Rafa nodded. "True. I guess I'm still kind of keyed into doing things right—the idea that you might not like something I'm doing set me off. Way off, apparently. I'll try to watch that tendency."

"Good—I guarantee it will make your life easier! I believe in preventing problems rather than curing them. I think a proactive check-in—like this one—is the most effective way for us to keep on track. My last mentoring relationship would have benefited from a direct conversation about how things were going after the first three months. There were some things we both needed to put on the table, but we never got that far. It's one of the life lessons I learned from that experience. Now I am much more diligent about raising issues when they surface and not putting them off. You, I am glad to say, are reaping the benefit of all of that learning."

Rafa smiled.

"I just want to make sure that we're doing things that are working for both of us in an optimal way," Cynthia continued. "So, literally, it is a check-in. I thought you had put it on your calendar when we talked about doing this a couple of months ago. It probably slipped your mind."

"I appreciate the clarification. It's probably a good leadership message for me, especially someday when I become someone's boss. You know, to do a check-in up front rather than wait."

"It's a real shortcut to good results. It's becoming more and more clear to me how difficult it can be for any employee to give feedback to someone who is senior to them in the organization. Rafa, I really do want to make sure that I'm supporting you and your learning, and that I'm doing it in the best way possible—which is why your feedback to me is invaluable.

"So," she said, leaning back in her chair, "do you feel better about the check-in now?"

"I do," said Rafa. "And if you don't mind, let's stick to the agenda as it is. OK?"

"OK."

"Good. So let's start off with *The Five Dysfunctions of a Team*."

"You were right on about *The Five Dysfunctions*, Cynthia. It was an easy book to read and actually hard to put down. The five-part model of team dysfunctions really made a huge impression."

"I've heard many people say the same thing," said Cynthia. "That little fable definitely captures some basic truths about group dynamics.

"So which of the five dysfunctions did you see as most relevant to your situation?" Cynthia asked.

"I think it's the second dysfunction, productive conflict," Rafa responded. "Our group is passive-aggressive."

"In what way?"

"Wally will present a plan or ask us for ideas, and we all nod our heads and agree," he explained. "And then the behind-the-scenes post-meeting takes place—you know, the parking lot conversations, where everyone disagrees with what Wally said and complains about it. I've always wondered why these guys didn't speak up during the meeting where they can actually get heard.

It's frustrating, because I am someone who does speak up. But when I do, I always get the 'OK, sure, that's fine, sounds good to me' stuff. I thought their acknowledgment was real, so naturally, I was looking for commitment and follow-through from the group, which never materialized. So there was always, as Lencioni calls it, 'confusion.' Well, I was certainly confused. I see now that I never really had their commitment, and now I understand why."

"And what would you say that reason is, according to Lencioni?"

"Because there's no sense of trust, and no sense of feeling safe," Rafa said. "People aren't willing to risk being vulnerable by taking a position, especially when it comes to disagreeing. You know—that 'productive conflict' he talks about. I completely agree that you need to be able to counter someone's idea or challenge the data, but our team is all about getting along. So we play the artificial harmony game—that is, until the meeting is over. Then the complaining begins. Once there is no one in earshot who matters, they grouse about any new idea."

"Rafa, I have a question for you. You say you speak up in your meetings, but it sounds like you get the same results that Wally does. I am pretty sure you aren't asking the group for consensus. Why do you think you get the same reaction?"

"I don't ask for consensus, but I do expect them to support my ideas. They don't offer any, and I do. I have been frustrated that they don't say, 'Good idea, Rafa.' They don't really say anything. But afterwards, they bash the idea among themselves. I think they don't do it at the table because they are afraid. I admit, I can be pretty direct and blunt, and I guess that intimidates them. So they stay quiet. It's easier, I guess."

Rafa let his gaze roam over the other diners as he thought more about his dilemma. In a quiet voice he said, "Maybe I'm bringing on the problem myself."

As if on cue, the waiter appeared with their food. Eating at Nikki's was a real treat. Rafa loved a good lasagna, and Nikki's was the best.

Cynthia was heartened—Rafa was beginning to realize that he was part of the problem, a good first step toward change. She decided to share some challenges that she had faced in dealing with the same issue. "Rafa," she said, putting down her fork, "you're not the first leader to come to this conclusion."

He looked up, curious.

"When I first took the helm of the department at CTBN, I was tasked with turning around a team that basically said 'This is the way we have always done it, and we're not changing for you.' I was frustrated by their lack of participation, and appalled by all the sabotage and negativity going on behind my back. This was not what I had expected to step into, and I had no idea what I could do, short of admitting defeat. It was Frank who suggested that I read *The Five Dysfunctions of a Team*. I did, and like you, I was relieved to find that I wasn't the only one in this boat. We discussed the parallels between that situation and my own team, and eventually I arrived at the same insight you did: I was contributing to the problem. It was pretty humbling."

"Yeah," Rafa nodded, "it is. So what did you do?"

"Well," said Cynthia, "I ended up giving each member of my management team a copy of the book. During weekly staff meetings, team members took turns facilitating discussions about each chapter. I took a backseat during those discussions, disciplining myself to listen rather than talk—which was not easy, believe me! But it worked. These discussions generated plenty of robust dialogue and deep insight, and they were able to identify specific themes that related to what was going on for our team. Eventually, we all worked collaboratively to strategize what we could do to turn things around."

Rafa made some notes after she spoke, and Cynthia took the opportunity to continue enjoying her meal. "You've given me some great ideas," said Rafa.

"Like what?" asked Cynthia.

"Well, it's clear that I can't control the group. I can't force them to participate. But if I lay back a little like you did, it might get them more engaged. So here's my takeaway from this whole discussion. Number one, when people feel afraid or intimidated, they aren't going to speak up, so you have to make it safe. Number two, if it's just your idea and nothing is coming from the team, it's easier for them to resist and disagree rather than support the idea, since they don't have any incentive to do otherwise. And number three, you have to get your team to generate the ideas so they will have ownership. Then they'll actually want to implement the ideas rather than feel they have to do it."

––––––––––

Cynthia was impressed—Rafa was a quick study. She dug into her Caesar salad as Rafa moved on to the second agenda item, an update on his status with Tom Seligman. "How is that going?" she asked.

"Amazing. Thanks again for connecting us. We're actually finalizing a time to meet again in three weeks."

"I'm so glad it went well."

"Yeah—he's a super guy. We met for thirty minutes or so, and he gave me a brief rundown on his change efforts and he suggested that I read this book *Switch: How to Change Things When Change Is Hard*. Do you believe it? Another book!" Rafa laughed. "I think this book is also going to be interesting and very applicable to my issues. Can you believe it? I'm becoming a reader! I will have read more books during this last month than I have in a year. And I'm seeing a real benefit. These books give you practical models and solutions to apply to issues you are actually experiencing. I had no idea."

"The book sounds interesting," said Cynthia. "You know, I haven't read that one. Maybe I'll read it too, and then next time we can discuss it."

"That would be awesome," said Rafa, "but are you sure? I don't want to take up even more of your time than you're already giving me—"

"No worries," said Cynthia. "I'm always on the lookout for good practical resources to boost my own leadership performance and pass on to future leaders. Believe it or not," she laughed, "I actually don't have all the answers."

"So," Cynthia prompted, "what's next on your agenda?"

"Formulating SMART goals. On the top of my list is listening. I'm trying to be very intentional—your word—when people are speaking to me. And I'm working on becoming a good listener, paying attention to what they're saying and responding to that. I'm not making snarky comments anymore, and I'm not judging other peoples' ideas in my head or just tapping my foot until it's my turn to talk. So that's a good thing, don't you think?"

"Definitely. Is it making a difference?"

"Well, not yet with anyone else, but I do see the difference in myself. Like, for one thing, I find that I understand other people's positions a lot better, and sometimes I get some new ideas. My attitude is much more positive. I am trusting that all this effort will eventually pay off, but I tell you, it is just plain exhausting. I have to work hard at it."

"Change is hard, hard is good, right?" She smiled. "I hope you keep it up. What about your other goals?"

"Well, 'not taking it personally' is a really tough one to pull off. I am consciously pausing before I react—you know, trying to be open, hold myself in check, so I don't immediately push back on someone else's ideas. I'm also working on suppressing the urge to start with the word "but" when I respond to other peoples' suggestions. Even when I disagree, I am still trying to understand their point of view. It makes me have to ask questions and challenge my assumptions."

"How does that work?"

Rafa replied without hesitation. "Last week one of my coworkers was presenting this proposal for a new way to calculate overtime compensation. Normally, I would have jumped in and immediately pointed out the flaws in his presentation. I was trying hard to be conscious of my listening goal, so I asked questions instead: 'How did you go about determining an average rate? What were you basing your margins on? Why didn't you include the second-shift employees in your proposal?' And, guess what? I got good responses. In fact, I got clarity on an issue that I had totally misunderstood. And one of my questions helped the guy see there was something he had overlooked." Rafa smiled, shaking his head in mock disbelief. "He even thanked me for asking the question!"

Cynthia was pleased to hear how diligent Rafa had been about working on his goals. It was great to see that he was getting some early payoff for his efforts.

As she praised his efforts, Rafa beamed with pride. Then his expression changed abruptly. "Thanks, but I'm far from perfect. I have to confess, there have been some lapses. Like this past week, I got into a heated argument with one of my coworkers, Todd, over a project I have been working on for a long time that he had botched. All my good intentions basically went out the window. He screwed up big time and wouldn't own it. I just went ballistic. But can you blame me? So much time and effort wasted, and he was oblivious. So I am sure I did everything wrong on my list. I know he was upset in the end."

"Well, when things cooled down, what did you do?" asked Cynthia.

"What do you mean?"

"Well, if you did something you didn't intend to do and it worked out badly, shouldn't you clean up your mess? Did you apologize, at least?"

Rafa put down his fork and pointed to his chest. "Me apologize? He made a huge mistake that affected *my* whole project. OK, so I blurted something maybe I shouldn't have; someone got offended, but then it was over. D-O-N-E! *I* have to apologize? It was his screw-up, and I had to make the fix." Rafa's tone was getting louder and more insistent.

"Wow," said Cynthia, looking around. "Cool it. *Shhhh* . . . Quiet down, Rafa. I can see you're really upset by this. You're getting all worked up."

"Yeah, sorry, I am upset. I am worked up. Why do I have to grovel when someone else made the mess and—"

"Back up," Cynthia interrupted. "Groveling? Do you call regretting that you lost your temper or embarrassed someone in a meeting, 'groveling'? That seems like a pretty extreme reaction. Is it possible, do you think, that you're so upset now because you know you were out of line before and you feel bad about it?"

Cynthia knew she was taking a risk in asking the question, but decided that if she didn't speak up and challenge his thinking, he might not realize how much he was contributing to the problem. She was aware that her comments might add a layer of tension between them.

Rafa folded his arms across his chest and clenched his jaw.

When it was clear that he wasn't ready to respond, Cynthia continued, "Mistake or not, you already said your good intentions went out the door. What would happen, for example, if you shared your real intentions with him? It might be useful to let Todd know that what transpired wasn't something you were proud of, and that you regretted reacting to the news of the project results in that way. What do you think?"

Rafa listened in silence. Cynthia hoped he was taking in what she had to say, but she wasn't sure. She pushed on. "Remember our own debate a few weeks back about being right or wrong?"

"I do, I do," Rafa said, pushing out the words. "You know, I am trying, but I'm not going to be perfect. Things happen." *What does she expect me to say to Todd? He's going to think I'm an idiot.*

"I am certainly not going to insist you apologize, Rafa. That's not my role. It is your decision. What I am doing is suggesting that you might benefit from talking to Todd face-to-face and expressing what you really intended to do. It's a start at least.

And it's practical: you have to work together every day—it would at least help clear the air between you."

"Yeah, I'll think about it . . . Listen, I know you're right. Sometimes I get really dug in to that right-wrong thing. I didn't even see it that way. It's just my go-to reaction. Another goal." Rafa let out a big sigh.

"Try to do it as soon as you can—before he runs off and tells six other people what you said to him. Or worse, fires off an email to his colleagues."

"I know, I know. It happens all the time."

"It happens to all of us. When someone feels hurt or injured by someone else's words or actions, they run to others for support. They get to tell their story to everyone who will listen. In their version, by the way, they are always the hero and we are villain. But genuine apologies really disarm people—you'll be surprised. Think about it, Rafa. Even though it has been a while, there's no time like the present."

"This is another example of one of those conversations I dread. It takes me out of my comfort zone. I know, I know, Cynthia, you're going to say, 'Good!'"

"I was." She smiled. "I think we've gotten to know each other well in the last three months!"

"OK," said Cynthia, "what's next? What progress have you made moving the team into the consultant role?"

Rafa presented his plan for moving forward on his goal, growing more and more enthusiastic as he related how he had approached the financial analysts individually. He asked each of them to meet with their internal clients to ask what additional support and resources they thought might help them better forecast their business results.

"That's where we are right now. My next step is to ask each FA to present their results and generate a list of priority services we could be providing. My intention is to get the team engaged. I want to get their buy-in early on. I'm trying my best to make the team cohesive by using a process to bring people together."

"So how is it working out for you?"

"Well, it seems to be working better. I expected a lot of flack, but I didn't get any. I was pleasantly surprised."

"I like your approach. I wonder . . ." Cynthia mused. "How do you think the 'old Rafa' would have handled this challenge?"

"The old Rafa probably would have gathered all the data himself," he said. "No doubt I would have met with and interviewed my team members' clients without them knowing it, and then presented the results at a meeting. I would have also proposed the new service requirements. And, to be honest, I would have expected their buy-in and appreciation for all my hard work. If they gave me flack, I probably would have been angry and frustrated, and ultimately my actions would have created more resistance and friction. It seems so obvious from here . . ." *Oh, dude! I really have to apologize to Todd, don't I?*

As Cynthia listened to Rafa, she sensed that he was right on the cusp of distancing himself from some of the unproductive strategies that he habitually used for solving problems. She was glad to see that even while retelling his encounters, he was becoming more reflective about his own behavior. It was clear that he was gaining insights that translated into new, more effective approaches. He was already embracing behaviors that would produce more positive, better results for him in the future.

Right now, however, Rafa was pensive. "I have another problem, a pretty big one. In order to get to the next level we need to reposition ourselves as business consultants. We need a sound understanding about how to forecast, identify trends, recognize the implications of a loss or gain in production. But honestly, my own ego aside, not everyone on the team has the ability to provide the high level of financial consulting that Wally is expecting. I know these people, and I know their skills. And for a lot of them the next level is going to be a real stretch." He paused, thoughtful.

"Anyway, here's the problem: three or four people on our team have been with the company for, like, twenty years. They probably started out as bookkeepers and have morphed over time into the FA role. Truth is, they barely can do the work now in the limited role we do have. I am positive they don't have the ability or desire to do more. And I don't think they ever will. This may be something that I actually can't deliver on. Half of our team will never make the grade!" His knee began bouncing up and down under the table. "I even started to wonder if Wally was setting me up."

In a very calm voice, she tried to get him to refocus. "What do you propose, then?"

"I know I could be successful if I had just the top three or four performers to work with!"

"Well, Rafa, maybe that's because you are thinking it's all or nothing—that it won't work because you can't get the whole team on board. Right?"

"Yeah, that's how I see it."

"Can't you meet him halfway, Rafa? Can't you start with the top four you mentioned and get them on board first?"

"Wait—you mean propose that we start by getting the top four on board first?"

"Why not? Don't worry as much about the group behind them. Maybe they will eventually surprise you. Perhaps eventually there will be two levels of the financial analyst position, those who can move forward and provide advance services and those who can't. The ones who can't move forward will stay at the entry level; the others can grow their skills and abilities and strive to become financial consultants. Maybe it's an internal designation, but maybe we can get it approved by HR and formalize it. Salary increases and all that. What do you think about that?"

"It sounds like a great idea. I can see the advantages. I can tell Wally that I'm going to start with a small group, begin there—kind of like a pilot program. Maybe I will never even have to get to the nonperformers. But it won't matter as much then, because we will already be seeing success with the others. And by the time I have to confront Wally with the fact that there some people who just don't have the ability to move forward, I will have the first four FAs—the ones that I think are capable of being consultants—performing effectively. I like your idea. Plus, the idea of creating a new position to grow into. I really like that."

"I think it has some real merit. How do you think Wally will take it, Rafa? And we have to think about how to get HR to approve it. That's the real concern."

"I don't know how Wally will respond, but it's worth a try."

"I think if you position it in the right way, he may surprise you and react favorably."

"What's the right way, in your opinion?"

"Well," said Cynthia, "let's brainstorm it." Together, they identified potential obstacles and roadblocks that could thwart Rafa's proposal. In the process, Cynthia shared a story about a strategy she had once used to get a new position in marketing approved through HR, and Rafa took copious notes.

When the waiter came to clear the table, Cynthia and Rafa ordered coffee and then turned to the last item on the agenda. "So, Rafa, the time has come for the dreaded check-in." She smiled. "Actually, this is something I think we should make a regular agenda item. And I promise it won't be too painful."

"OK—the check-in," Rafa said, looking at his notes. "Relationship, learning, and process, right? I'm not sure how to start this."

"Well, let's start with the relationship. Are you getting what you need from our mentoring relationship? For example, early on we talked about what we each wanted from this relationship. As your mentor, I want to make sure that I am giving you what you need."

"I think our relationship is great. Actually, Cynthia, it is really more than great, and much more than I expected. I would certainly never have been able to hold these kinds of honest, out-front conversations with my supervisor. With a mentor—with you, I mean—I feel much more comfortable. I can trust you. The confidentiality issue is a big deal to me. I know what I say stays between us. That helps me be more open and honest."

"Good. And I feel the same, especially about some of my perspectives on our mutual colleagues. So let's talk about the process—how we are working together, the amount of time, the working on goals? The reading, our conversations—how is that all going for you, Rafa?"

"Well, it all goes back to the trust thing. From the beginning, you've been sharing your stories with me. And they aren't about your big successes and accolades, but more about what you've learned as a result of your disappointments, problems, and challenges. I never thought of successful leaders as having a learning curve, I guess, so your stories inspire me. I grew up believing that you should never reveal your vulnerabilities because people will take advantage of you. As you well know by now, it's been ingrained in me since I first started playing baseball. But business is different than baseball."

He's come a long way in three months, Cynthia thought.

"Anyway," Rafa continued, "I can see the value of your approach. Your stories help me see that you're a real person, that you weren't always the perfect leader, and that made me trust you—which, by the way, is a huge aha! for me. I'm beginning to see the importance of having trust in my relationship with my team members, and maybe a way I can build it. Or rebuild it, in some cases."

"Thanks, Rafa. I'm glad that my stories have been helpful in shaping your thinking and sparking new ideas for you."

"But this process stuff has been hard. Having someone make me stop and deal with issues and questions and dig deeper all the time is agonizing, but I have to admit—it helps. A lot. On my own, I would never have gotten it. Now I'm starting to hear your voice in my head, like a coach. Or maybe a cheerleader."

Cynthia laughed. "So how about what you are learning from all of this? Let's talk about that."

"What am I learning? Well, for one thing, I had no idea that other people saw me as overly aggressive and intimidating. You know, in team sports—sorry, but this is relevant—guys are always facing off, blowing up, blowing off steam, and then it's over and we move on. But in the office I guess that kind of approach makes me the big bully. I know that physically I can be intimidating. And I can get loud. And that isn't an image I want to project . . ."

He drifted off, struck by what he was saying, then continued, "Anyway, you're helping me see that. And it's also pretty obvious that I have this drive to be right all the time, which really is impossible. And that just because someone else has a good point, that doesn't mean my idea is wrong. And vice versa. And that even if I make a bad decision, it doesn't mean that I am not good at my job. That's a lot! I wouldn't have said I was being defensive, but I guess I was and probably I still am, and I need to work on that."

"Those are all good things to figure out, Rafa. And the fact that you did it over such a short period of time is nothing short of amazing. Good job."

"Well, I've come to see that maybe I've been too much about me, being the big hero all the time. I have to do a better job of being about the 'we.' That's what I really have to work on. I think you helped me see that it isn't completely about changing myself, which I was afraid was going to be the message. I need to do a better job of leveraging my strengths." He paused. "I appreciate how you always make me feel like I bring something substantial to the table."

"That's because I believe in you," Cynthia replied. "You have a lot of talent worth developing. You work hard. You are really committed to your growth. I admire that. Actually, it's because you are so willing to invest time and energy that it inspires me, as a mentor, to do the same. I am impressed by your conscientiousness and your commitment to taking yourself and your team to the next level."

Rafa basked in her praise. "Thank you. Thank you. That means a lot."

"And, while I see your commitment, I hope you'll continue to show some patience for the process. Nothing in business happens overnight, believe me. I wonder if your drive to get results at work also shows up in how you work on your leadership goals."

"Are you saying I'm trying too hard?"

"No, I'm just wondering if you are measuring your leadership development by stats—by what you accomplish."

Rafa shrugged and cocked his head. "I'm not sure I get what you're saying."

"Well, the way I see it, you are driving yourself hard to do things. Listening, asking questions, the proposal plan with Wally. I just want to make sure you aren't just ticking off items on a checklist. Listening—check. Asking questions—check. That's not what I am looking for from you. As you work on your leadership development, I want you to remember that ultimately leadership is about building solid relationships and less about tasks, actions, and achievements."

She waited for a moment to see how Rafa would react before going on. "This may seem counterintuitive, but it is easier sometimes to 'do,' rather than to 'be.' I am asking you not to do leadership but to work at being a leader—to grow into the person who can deliver on your goal. That means developing yourself and cultivating relationships, and expanding your capacities, and strengthening your competencies as well."

"I do tend to focus on the doing. I will grant you that," Rafa said.

"I know. And early on, that's what gets rewarded, especially when you are an aspiring leader. The company likes results, but results take you only so far in your career development."

"Are you saying it's wrong to get results?"

"It isn't wrong, but alone it is insufficient. Nothing is sustainable without relationships. That was what Lencioni was saying in *The Five Dysfunctions*. Eventually, as you move up the ladder, you are going to have to motivate people to do the work, take on the tasks, and own their assignments. The only way you are going to be successful is to lead them and have them follow you. But people won't follow you if they don't think you care about them, or they don't feel you trust them, or if they don't trust you. That means building trust and strengthening relationships, which doesn't happen overnight. It takes time. It goes beyond a proposal, or a spreadsheet. It is more than all that. Much more."

"Wait—so you're saying that early on, it's more about you and your achievements and what you are doing. But later on, as a leader, you have to get people to work with you and be on board with you, and you have to be able to rely on them. And then it's less about your own actions and more about what your team is doing. Right?"

"Right."

"So am I at a place where I have to concentrate on the people side? Is that what you mean?"

"Yes, you've got it. Managers who move to leadership often struggle with this transition. They are more accustomed to performing and getting credit for their accomplishments. They often cling to tasks and struggle with delegation. Their supervisors find them working on the wrong things, with the wrong priorities, because they can't let go of what they know how to do and what has gotten them where they are today. Unfortunately, it won't take them to the next level. That's the issue."

"I think I see a bit of Wally in your description. He's still doing things that we think he should be passing down to us."

Cynthia was tired of hearing about Wally. She purposely shifted the direction of the discussion. "Rafa, one of the challenges for you down the road is to begin to think about making this shift. Our work together is in part to get you started on that."

"I am going to have to do some work there. I tend to focus on the concrete, not the warm, fuzzy stuff, I grant you. It will be a challenge."

They both paused, and Rafa tapped some quick notes into his tablet.

Cynthia took a deep breath. "Check-in goes both ways," she began. "Do you have some feedback for me?"

Rafa's surprise was obvious. "Feedback for you? Isn't that what I just did?"

"Feedback about my performance as a mentor—yes, I'd really appreciate it. Mentoring is always a work in progress, for both partners. Tell me what you think is working well, and then let's focus on what I could do better—or do more of, or less of—to support you."

Rafa froze. He wasn't about to say anything negative to his mentor, not this mentor, at any rate. He didn't want to jeopardize the relationship in any way. He had too much to lose. Besides, he wanted her to like him and continue to work with him. And then . . . he was always aware of the risk of saying something wrong to a senior executive that could come back to bite him later.

"Come on," said Cynthia, with a warm smile. "I am sure you have something to suggest."

"Really, it's all been great," he assured her.

"Thanks, but I know that can't possibly be true. Rafa, relax— this is where you get to help me. As I mentioned, I didn't have the best success last year with my mentee, and I think it was because there were things going on with her that never came out. I didn't pick up on her cues, which meant that I wasn't able to offer the best strategies to help her, and she quit before we'd barely gotten started. I really don't want that to happen again. So since you like me so much," she smiled, signaling her teasing, "let's focus this part of the conversation on helping me learn how to get better at this. This is for me."

"OK, OK." Rafa thought for a moment. "Cynthia, I do think you are a great mentor. You are awesome. Remember when I said that I felt lucky when we first met? I really didn't know how lucky I was until I spoke with some of my fellow Leadership NextGeners. It's clear that you are much more skilled than a lot of other mentors—some of my colleagues are still struggling to get dates on the calendar. One of them met with her mentor once and that's been it!"

He paused. "But . . . OK. Feedback. At first I found it annoying that I never got a straight answer from you. Instead, you always threw a question back at me. I've come to realize that you were trying to get me to think things through for myself. You were making me have to do the work. And you were either supporting my idea or offering another perspective. That was very ingenious of you—and effective, too, I might add. Now, even when we aren't scheduled to meet, I find myself posing a question out loud to myself. Like I said, it's like you are the voice in my head, and I find myself asking myself a Cynthia question. And then I try to work my way to an answer in the same way we do it together. I must say, it is pretty, pretty cool approach."

"And so is my coffee about now." Cynthia downed the rest of her coffee and offered Rafa her biscotti. She wasn't crazy about anise.

"Thanks," he said, dipping it into his coffee. "And, of course, your humor. Even when some of our conversations were heavy, you kept it light with your humor. I think that helped a lot early on to keep me more relaxed. So thanks for that."

"You're welcome. I think humor does help."

"And one more thing that I think you do that has worked particularly well: all the structural stuff you put in place early on. It seemed so formal and rigid at the time, it really freaked me out. But it has kept us—me—on track. We always have a date on the calendar. I routinely put together an agenda. So we have a time and a focus. I know you told me in the beginning that it would be helpful, but honestly, I didn't know what to expect about the mentoring thing, so it went right over my head. Now it makes all the sense in the world."

Cynthia probed further. "Do you have any suggestions about how I could have positioned it better, so as not to scare you?"

"I'm not sure. I know you told me early on that you had some relationships that floundered. Maybe if you'd been even more specific about how lack of time and commitment to a structure got in the way, that might have moved me along faster."

Cynthia jotted down a note to remind herself. "Rafa, that's a good idea, and a nice segue into the flip side. What else hasn't been as helpful for you?"

"This is a small point. I know that you are pushing me to be better, and I appreciate the push—but sometimes I feel overwhelmed with the assignments, the commitments, and the agenda. There's a lot on my plate besides this. I have a job I have to do. It might be helpful if you asked me about my workload and make sure I can handle everything you want to put on my plate."

"Good point. You're right. Sometimes I get so excited about what we are doing that I assign tasks without considering your work pressures. And I do know that being a mentee is not your full-time job. I will definitely keep that in mind." She jotted down another note.

Nice, Rafa thought. *She really takes what I have to say seriously.* "And here's a minor thing, but you told me to put together the agenda—that I was in the driver's seat and the agenda was on my plate."

"Yes, and—?"

"So your note about today's meeting? You essentially drafted the entire agenda. I know you wanted to introduce this check-in thing, but you also included everything else. So I felt a little like you were micromanaging. But it's a small thing."

"Duly noted." She looked up. "Was it really a small thing?"

"Well, it did bug me."

They both smiled.

"OK, thanks for being honest. Anything else?"

Rafa nodded and struggled for a moment to find the right words. "Well, it's about . . . you always seem to . . ."

Cynthia shot him a look: *Spit it out.*

"OK. When you introduced me to Tom as the 'young man,' or refer to me as a 'young man,' it's embarrassing. It makes me feel like a child. I can't help it that I'm young. I've got to start somewhere, I realize that. But young this and young that is irritating. It makes me feel like there's a wall and I can't climb over it until I reach the right age—it seems patronizing. That's really a hot button for me."

"Wow, I wasn't even aware I was doing that. Rafa, it took a lot of courage to say that. Thank you for doing that. I never realized how off-putting that would be for you. You won't be hearing me say that again, young man!"

Rafa looked startled. And then they both laughed.

"OK," said Cynthia. "So now that you are well on your way with some concrete goals, do you think that we should move to meeting once a month instead of every two weeks? Remember when we talked about assessing our frequency of meeting? This might be a good time to revisit our timetable. What do you think?"

"Is meeting less often something that is for me, or for you? Because even though I complain about all the work I have to do, if this is about what I need I would actually like to continue meeting every two weeks. That is, if you would be willing to still give me the time. I could use the guidance and support as I get this team challenge going. Plus, you keep me focused on the relationship stuff."

"If that's what you need, Rafa, sure. Let's keep this format going. Maybe we can reassess at our six-month check-in if it's still an issue. Agreed?"

"Agreed."

The restaurant was starting to empty after the lunch rush. "I think our time is up. What did you think of this meeting? Was it helpful?"

"Absolutely. You were right. The check-in wasn't painful. It was a good idea."

They both suddenly noticed the check on the table, and Cynthia reached for it immediately. "This one is on me, as promised."

"Thank you. I loved the food," he said with a satisfied grin, patting his stomach. "I haven't had a lasagna this good since the last time I was home, but don't tell my mom I said that. I always tell her there is no lasagna that even comes close to her lasagna, and that's the way she likes it."

Cynthia and Rafa walked out of the restaurant together. The bright Arizona sunlight took some adjusting to after sitting in the dark restaurant for so long. They had both worked hard and made good progress, and they were on their way to a new place in their relationship.

"Thanks for lunch, and thanks for the good conversation. I can't believe it's already been ninety days. We sure covered a lot of ground today. I'm actually exhausted," he confessed.

"It is hard work sometimes, isn't it?"

"Sometimes?" He rolled his eyes.

"But I guarantee it will be worth it when you 'go the distance.' See you in a couple of weeks."

Digging Deeper

Questions for Mentors:

1. The sixth meeting focused on checking in on the relationship. What are the advantages of having a regular check-in? Is that something you and your mentoring partners do periodically? If not, what gets in the way?

2. When told there was going to be a check-in, Rafa became worried and started to second-guess himself. (He had

forgotten that he and Cynthia had talked about it in their second meeting.) What could Cynthia have done to avoid having him get so worked up?

3. During the course of the meeting, Rafa and Cynthia discussed several books. What kinds of resources could you use (or have you used) to deepen the learning for your mentees?

4. There was a tense moment during the meeting when Cynthia challenged Rafa about his behavior with a colleague and the expectation of apologizing. How would you have handled this situation? Would you have been as direct as Cynthia?

5. Cynthia tells Rafa, "I believe in you. You have a lot of talent worth developing." When was the last time you gave your mentees positive feedback? What did you say?

6. Cynthia asked Rafa—pushed him, in fact—to give her some feedback about what she could do better as a mentor. Rafa was reluctant to say anything that might negatively impact their relationship. Have you asked your mentees to give you feedback? What more can you do or say to encourage your mentees to give you honest feedback?

Questions for Mentees:

1. The sixth mentoring meeting focused on checking in on the relationship. What are the advantages of having a regular check-in? Is that something you and your mentoring partner do periodically? If not, what gets in the way?

2. When told there was going to be a check-in, Rafa became worried and started to second-guess himself. What could Cynthia have done to avoid having him get so worked up?

3. During the course of the meeting, Rafa and Cynthia discussed several books. What sorts of resources would you like to have your mentor suggest?

4. Cynthia tells Rafa, "I believe in you. You have a lot of talent worth developing." When was the last time your mentor gave

you positive feedback? What did he or she say? How did you respond?

5. How do you think your mentor would rate her satisfaction level with your progress? How might you go about finding out?

6. Cynthia asked Rafa—pushed him, in fact—to give her some feedback about what she could do better as a mentor. Rafa was reluctant to say anything that might negatively impact their relationship. What feedback would you like to give to your mentor? What do you need to do to get comfortable giving that feedback?

Epilogue: Five Years Later

The auditorium was buzzing with conversation as CTBN employees filed in and took their seats. Cynthia sat next to Rafa, who was engrossed in a conversation with a coworker. She didn't intend to eavesdrop, but she couldn't help overhearing their conversation.

"So, I guess I'm not sure where to go from here. You always seem to know just how to handle things . . . Look, Rafa, I know you don't have a lot of extra time, but if we could just meet for fifteen minutes or so it might really help me figure a way out of this."

"Sure, no problem," Rafa said. "Shoot me an email and we'll set up a time."

Five years, Cynthia thought. *It's been an interesting journey for both of us . . .*

Three months after their ninety-day check-in, they'd cut back to monthly meetings. Rafa had proposed the new financial analyst position to Wally, and he had jumped on it.

The two of them began to meet regularly with HR to make the case, formulate the job description, and determine the pay structure. While it was being approved, Rafa got busy. He worked on designing training modules to align with the responsibilities of the new position, consulted with team members on the topics and issues they wanted to address, and collaborated with them in launching the rollout. When the curriculum was completed, he was pleased to see that three of his six coworkers had signed up for the training he would be delivering. HR finally signed off on the new position in August, and Wally immediately promoted Rafa into it.

All this had happened in less than a year since their mentoring relationship had begun, and Cynthia had been impressed.

He'd taken mentoring seriously, reflected on his path, and used what he'd learned. And, she was pleased to see, he'd grown much more comfortable with himself and with her. Cynthia recalled a conversation that had occurred about eleven months into their relationship. As they neared the end of the session, they had discussed the agenda for their next and final meeting. Cynthia reminded Rafa that the NextGen Leadership Mentoring Program would be coming to a close at the end of December, and she asked about how he wanted to spend the time.

"Well, ideally," he joked, "I'd like to spend it watching a spring training game."

They had a good laugh over that suggestion. By that point, it had been some time since Rafa had mentioned baseball, and Cynthia knew that he was making fun of himself. Although it would have been a perfect closure to the year, it was impossible— the Cactus League wouldn't start for another three months. Instead, Cynthia suggested they use their last meeting to review the year and talk about what they each had learned from the process and the progress they made. Rafa laughed. "Oh, I get it—it's one of your check-ins again!"

At their December meeting they had held their closure conversation—the official end of their formal mentoring relationship. She acknowledged the personal satisfaction she'd gotten from watching Rafa grow and develop over the year. She reaffirmed what she had said many times during recent months, that she was impressed with his commitment to his own development. "The energy and effort you've consistently put into our mentoring relationship inspired me to work harder to make it more meaningful for both of us. I have to admit than when we first met, I didn't think you would turn out to be so self-aware. But then I could see that it was more of a habit you'd fallen into, and that your fixation on your baseball training and your injury was holding you back from being more open and real with your coworkers. And I knew from our relationship, the way you accepted and acted on my feedback even when you didn't like it, that you were more than capable of change."

Rafa laughed. "Yeah, you really laid into me a few times. But nicely, of course!"

"Of course! And you did everything I asked of you, once you understood where we were heading with all of it—the readings, the interviews, and the feedback, and then some—with real commitment. You weren't just going through the motions to satisfy me. I truly appreciated your enthusiasm for learning and growing. Between you and me, not every mentee is like you."

Rafa blushed at the compliment, but Cynthia was still talking. "So that's my two cents. I'd love to hear your perspective on the year."

"I knew we'd be talking about this," he began, "so I reread the notes that I wrote a year ago. It was a humbling experience, to say the least. I was so cocky. Even though I wanted help, I still thought I had all the answers. And I was really defensive."

They laughed, but then Rafa became serious. "I was so irritated when you made me assess my strengths and weaknesses—I saw it as a writing assignment. But knowing what I know now, it makes me even more appreciative of you and the patience you've shown as my mentor. I thought it would be a snap—I'd tell you my issues, you'd tell me what to do, I'd have a promotion in two weeks. Not. I feel like I've learned years of knowledge in twelve months, maybe because it was such a rough journey for me."

"What in particular did you find rough?"

"Well, I was put off by all the structure you insisted on at the beginning. I didn't see what it was for—why couldn't we just talk without all that formality? And I definitely did not understand, going in, that mentoring was about introspection and reflection—I didn't even know what those words meant. And that it wasn't just about you telling me what to do. It actually required me to be fully on board."

"Which you have done beautifully, I would say."

"Thanks." But Rafa wasn't finished. "The honesty thing was huge for me, sharing my vulnerabilities . . . being honest with myself was the hardest part, seeing that half the time the reason I wasn't moving forward was because I was standing in my own way. I remember that first time, when you challenged me on my baseball talk. Anyone else, I probably would have just quit. But you made me feel like you were on my side. And you shared your own career challenges, which was awesome. After that, I guess I was more open to what you had to say, like about my need to be right all the time." Rafa raised his eyebrows and smiled: "You were right about that, by the way.

"And your introduction to Tom Seligman was on target. I'm still working off of his ideas on initiating an organizational change. But the biggest thing you helped me discover was that you can't lead effectively without building and strengthening relationships. I came into mentoring convinced that it was all about achievement and visibility, just like in baseball. Putting the emphasis on people and trust shifted my perspective. And beginning with the end in mind put me on the right course. Instead of expecting everyone else to validate my ideas, I started validating others' ideas—when I agreed with them, of course. And then I realized that when I did, they were more likely to listen to what I had to say in return. Big takeaway. 'Begin with the end in mind' is a good philosophy for a leader, and I have you to thank for that."

And then Rafa removed a small, wrapped package from his coat pocket and placed it in front of her. She looked at the gift at first curiously and then apprehensively. Rafa had told her that he wanted to give her something to remind her of their year together, to show his appreciation for her time and energy, and mostly to say thank you for all she had done to help him. Cynthia had been tempted to tell him that she didn't need to be thanked, but then she remembered how important it had been for her to thank Frank for his time.

She unwrapped the package carefully and smiled as she pulled out a small silver frame around the beautifully printed quote: "Begin with the End in Mind."

Cynthia was deeply touched, and she told Rafa how much she appreciated the gift. "I'm going to put it on the shelf behind my desk so that my future mentees will be sure to see it!" She could imagine them repeating the words to themselves, just as Rafa had done, and that would be her cue to relate the story about how one mentee used it to remind himself to make a difference in the way he interacted with his team . . .

———

In the auditorium, Rafa finished up his conversation with his coworker and turned to Cynthia. "You look deep in thought."

"I was just thinking about how time flies, Rafa. You've done so well!"

Over the few years that followed their mentorship, Rafa's career had moved steadily upward, yet he'd begun to see that as much as he had learned, there was still a lot he didn't know. He had begun to think about working out a way to get an executive MBA degree, and he'd bounced the idea off of Cynthia at one of their lunch meetings. "I think I heard your voice in my head when it occurred to me," he had said, laughing.

"That's an interesting idea . . . I hope I didn't give you the idea that our mentoring sessions were all about getting you back to school—"

"Oh no. It's more that I'm still trying to think of how I want my career to look in the future. Just because I actually got the job I wanted, I know I'm not done with my development. I'd really like to tap my full potential, not just finesse my way from project to project."

Rafa had gone back for his executive MBA, and he'd worked hard to juggle his studying and workload. He was never sure whether the new degree had anything to do with it, but two years after his first promotion he had received another promotion. Now, as he sat next to Cynthia, he felt like they were almost colleagues.

"You've done well over the last few years too, Cynthia." Three years previously, the company had reconfigured its miniature audio amplification devices to fit smartphones and tablets, and Cynthia had launched an award-winning marketing campaign. Within several months, sales had tripled even the most optimistic forecasts. Cynthia had been promoted to the position of executive vice president, acquired a larger office with an even better panoramic view, and switched to luxury French chocolates, Maison de Chocolat.

"I have," she replied. "We've had some big wins! Oh—congratulations! I heard that the NextGen coordinator asked you to mentor a new graduate of the program."

Rafa laughed. "Role reversal, huh? It's great, actually. I'm excited about the opportunity to give back and pay it forward, but I want to get it right." He paused. "I'll definitely have to consult with you to get some pointers."

"I'd be happy to do that. I learned so much from being your mentor."

This led Cynthia to reflect on how she'd changed, She had certainly become more self-aware. Like Rafa, she had learned that she had to break down the perception that she was an intimidating person. Apparently that just came with her position in the company. Mentoring Rafa had helped her see that she, too, needed to take time to build relationships, to do more listening and less talking, and to continue asking questions that invite feedback. Listening had always been a challenge for her, and it was still a work in progress. As a result of her experience with Rafa, she was far more comfortable and adept at giving feedback to her own staff, and they had become more forthright with her as a result.

She came out of her reverie to the sound of Rafa's voice.

"Cynthia—remember those books you introduced me to? Well, you won't believe it, but I actually read a few books a year now."

"Really? What are you reading now?"

Rafa gave her a sheepish grin. "*Moneyball*, of course."

Cynthia laughed. "Sounds perfect."

A sudden flurry of activity at the front of the auditorium caught their attention. Wally, several senior executives, and three of the CTBN founding brothers—Carl, Thomas, and Barry—stepped up onto the stage and sat down on the chairs behind the podium. CTBN's CEO, Randy Reston, approached the podium, leaned into the microphone, and announced that the program was about to begin. The crowd hushed. It was Wally's retirement, and everyone was gathered there to honor him.

Several speeches and a few gifts and many photographs later, it was Wally's turn to address the group. Gingerly, he stepped up to the microphone. It was clear that he was uncomfortable being in the limelight, and he stuttered and stumbled at first. Even though public speaking was not his forte, the emotion that showed on his face was stirring. Anyone could see that he was touched by the outpouring of all the compliments and good wishes.

Wally looked lovingly at his wife and children sitting in the front row, not far from Cynthia and Rafa. He thanked his family for their unswerving support and their patience as he put his work and CTBN first, especially during the early years. Wally cast his gaze over all the employees sitting before him. He spoke about the great company that they all had the privilege to be working for, and he encouraged them to take advantage of the opportunities they had been afforded. He reminded them that no one was going to hand them a career: they owned their own careers, and they each had a responsibility to make that career happen. He challenged them to push back, to ask for what they needed, offer suggestions, commit to making things better, and work on their own development.

Wally paused during the enthusiastic applause that followed, and then slowly turned his head toward the first few rows, where his finance department staff was sitting. As he spoke, he looked them each directly in the eye and told them how proud he was of his talented, dedicated, and committed team—and added that it had been a real privilege to work with a team that was willing to do what it took to get the job done. Many in the audience dabbed at tears welling up in their eyes.

Wally took a sip of water, heaved a sigh, and slowly looked back out at the crowd. "So, the day has come, my friends. Finally, after forty-two years, I am retiring from CTBN. And I confess—I've dreaded it. What made this decision easier for me is that we now have a talented leader who is ready to step in and take our finance department to the next level."

He paused and then beamed. "Ladies and gentlemen, I want to take this opportunity to announce my successor—a man who has the vision, the energy, the determination, and the foresight to move us forward into the future. Rafa Moretti, will you join me at the podium, please?"

Rafa stood and, once again, stepped up to the plate.

Cynthia's and Rafa's Advice for Mentors and Mentees

Cynthia and Rafa both benefited from their mentoring relationship. The first ninety days stimulated especially significant learning time for both of them. Here's the essence of what each took away from the experience, and what they would pass on to others who find themselves working with a new mentoring partner.

What Cynthia Learned from Mentoring Rafa

One of the things I like best about my role as a mentor is that I learn from my mentees just as they learn from me. My goal each time is to capture what I learned and apply it to my next relationship. My experience with Rafa reinforced some of what I had experienced with other mentees, but it also taught me some new things I can draw on when I work with new mentees.

Before we met, I spent time thinking about the fears and anxieties I experienced early on in my career when I was trying to make my mark. **My *tip*: Try walking in your mentee's shoes. It will help you better understand where he is coming from.**

I knew that my senior position might create a barrier to honest conversation, so I tried to make Rafa as comfortable as possible and get him talking about himself. **My *tip*: Remove power and position barriers by being personable, open, and interested in your mentee.**

Rafa had a somewhat skewed understanding of what mentoring is and how he saw my role as his mentor. We spent time clarifying our roles and responsibilities before we really got into mentoring. **My *tip*: Don't assume you and your mentee understand mentoring in the same way. Share your viewpoints and come to a mutual understanding.**

Listening has always been a challenge for me. Rafa came to meetings with lots of questions, and it would have been easy for me to give him answers. I had to remind myself that what Rafa really wanted, even if he didn't know it, was to discover answers for himself. **My *tip*: Fight the instinct to give your mentee answers. Concentrate instead on asking questions that take their thinking deeper.**

At the start, we were on a honeymoon. We both wanted to like each other, be liked, and enjoy meeting. I had to interrupt the honeymoon once issues arose that got in Rafa's way. **My *tip*: You must be frank and honest with your mentees if you want them to grow—it's essential for your relationship if it is going to progress.**

Rafa frequently got caught up in his current work issues. Although they were opportunities for learning, they could have dominated our meeting time. I had to be disciplined about our time and periodically get us refocused. **My *tip*: Don't get lost in day-to-day issues. They can easily distract you from working on development goals, the real focus of mentoring.**

Each time I met with Rafa, I ended up learning something. I found that I had better recall of what we had covered when I jotted down my observations and insights at the end of each meeting. **My *tip*: Increase your learning and retention by capturing insights after a mentoring meeting.**

Rafa needed to conduct some difficult conversations that made him quite uncomfortable. I held him accountable for undertaking them, but I also helped him feel more competent and confident by coaching him through his approach. **My *tip*: To help your mentees gain more confidence and** competency, don't be afraid to push them out of their comfort zone.

When I raised the issue of Rafa's baseball obsession, I was unsure whether I might be jeopardizing the relationship by crossing the line. **My *tip*: Engage in meaningful conversations, but remember that you are not your mentee's therapist.**

I made a few mistakes with Rafa, and I was lucky that he had the courage to speak up and tell me about them. It was my job to make sure I accepted the feedback without being defensive. **My *tip*: Mentors aren't perfect. If you make a mistake or disappoint your mentee, apologize and learn from it.**

What Rafa Learned from Cynthia

The payoff was enormous, but mentoring turned out to be harder work than I thought it would be going in. Looking back, I had a lot of misconceptions about what the whole process was about. These are my ten best tips for new mentees—things I wish I had known going in.

1. Mentoring is all about trust. You've got to trust your mentor, and you also have to trust yourself enough to trust someone else.

2. You may come into mentoring with your own mindset and your own "truth," but you are likely to discover new perspectives and multiple truths pretty quickly.

3. Mentoring can have a profound impact on your personal growth, but you have to be willing to be open to change and authentic about yourself.

4. The focus of mentoring is on learning and growing. Don't fixate on immediate achievement. Mentoring is about developing your future potential.

5. Good mentors don't just give you answers. They ask tough questions and expect you to do your share of the heavy lifting.

6. Mentors expect their investment in you to pay off. Stay on top of things by being accountable.

7. Real growth comes when you are pushed out of your comfort zone. If you're uncomfortable, that's probably a good thing.

8. Mentoring isn't just showing up for meetings. It requires effort and a serious investment of your time and energy, so make sure it's a top priority and serious commitment.

9. What you learn in a mentoring relationship applies to other relationships as well. Look for ways to leverage your insights.

10. Mentoring is not your ticket to promotion—it's your opportunity to become promotable.

Part Two

The Mentoring
Conversation Playbook

Moving the Conversation from Monologue to Dialogue

M ost of us have experienced that rare moment when a quick chat suddenly turns into something far more profound. Instead of talking *at* each other, we are actively listening *to* each other; rather than exchanging information, we are engaging in authentic sharing. It is only when there is mutual respect and openness to different points of view that we feel safe conversing at this level. We understand that what is shared inside the conversation will remain between us. These moments of mutual trust trigger new insights and deeper relationships. This is the transformative power of good conversation, and the foundation of a productive mentoring partnership.

The Five Levels of Conversation

The Levels of Conversation Model (Figure 10.1) illustrates the five levels of conversation and their relationship to building trust and promoting learning in a mentoring relationship. As you can see, mentoring conversations are built on a foundation of trust; and learning increases as the conversation moves from basic information transaction to a genuine collaboration and dialogue. Use this model to help figure out where you are in your own conversations, and where you want to be.

Level 1: Monologue

Monologue is essentially a nonconversation in which one party claims all the airspace for storytelling, lecturing, or expounding. It rarely builds trust or promotes learning, and it shuts down any opportunity for a real exchange of ideas.

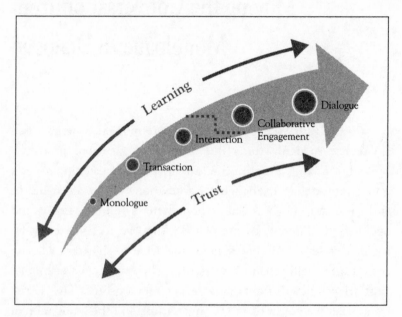

Figure 10.1 Levels of Conversation

Some mentors view their role as "sage on the stage"—the more traditional perception of mentoring. They fill most of their mentoring meetings with monologue, relating their personal war stories and instructing the mentee about what they need to know, learn, and do. The mentee is expected to take notes, then go off and follow suit.

As a result, there is little room for the mentee's voice, critical thinking, or exploration. Because the mentee lacks a personal investment in the conversation, there is no sense of partnership, much less ownership.

Level 2: Transaction

Most people who profess to be in conversation are actually engaging in transaction. Their discussion goes back and forth, but it always remains on the surface:

"Have you met with your supervisor yet?"

"Yes. We had a great conversation."

"Good to hear it. So have you developed some goals as a result?"

"No. I haven't had any time."

"How about the self-assessment? Have you had time for that??"

"I'm working on it. It is coming slowly. Maybe I'll have something to show you by next week."

Mentoring relationships that are stuck in transaction run the risk of becoming a series of text messages instead of real conversations. Every yes-or-no question is a dead end, and both partners soon exhaust the well of conversation. Once the mentee feels that she has gotten as much as she can from the mentor, she loses energy to continue. The relationship ends with both parties feeling dissatisfied and relieved that it is over.

Level 3: Interaction

Interaction looks and feels a lot more like conversation than monologue and transaction. As such, it can fool you into thinking you've reached your conversation level goal, so it's important to understand the limitations and uses of this conversation style.

Many mentors and mentees begin their relationship by exchanging personal information and career stories. These interactions are useful and important information exchanges, but they usually skim the surface and turn into a kind of Q&A session: Your mentee asks you how to get something done, and you respond by suggesting different ways to do it. Your mentee asks you about which leadership qualities you think are important to get to the next level, and you respond with a list of the characteristics you deem critical for success. Your mentee leaves the session with an interesting list of things to do or ways to behave, but he has not discovered these new ideas for himself.

Because interaction feels so much like conversation, it's comfortable. The unfortunate result is that it becomes a habit, and that rarely produces significant growth and development. Once you leave the safe harbor of interaction, the quality of the interaction shifts. Now you can do the work of mentoring.

Level 4: Collaborative Engagement

Collaborative engagement is where deeper insight and reflection take place. Because trust has been established, mentor and mentee are both willing to be vulnerable with each other. For example:

The mentee shares his personal fear and discomfort about making a presentation in front of his peers and senior leaders. "I'm afraid they're not going to take me seriously."

The mentor responds, "I remember feeling the same way when I got promoted and had to make a presentation in front of senior leadership. I was trying to prove that I was smart enough to be in the role. I think by trying to prove myself, rather than talking about what I knew, I was working too hard, and it showed."

The mentee is surprised to hear this. "But you are such a natural speaker now. How did you get there?"

The mentor uses this question to jump-start a collaborative learning opportunity: "I wish I could say it was an easy journey. I had to work at it, and I know you will too. But that's something we can take on together."

When mentoring partners are willing to be vulnerable, trust is deepened and the relationship is strengthened. The mentor learns something new about the mentee, and the mentee begins to understand that the mentor is a person who also struggled in creating her own career path. This kind of insight helps the mentee feel confident in that, with some work, he can indeed move forward toward achieving a goal. Now learning can accelerate, taking the partnership to a whole new level.

Level 5: Dialogue

It is a special moment when mentoring conversations reach a level of dialogue that leads to transformational thinking. On this level, conversation partners are interested only in learning, exploring, and understanding; there is no debate, no attempt to convince or change the other person's mind about something.

The fruits of dialogue are huge: discovery and transformative learning.

When conversation becomes dialogue, shared understanding arises from the mutual learning that is taking place. Because trust is high, it allows an open exchange of ideas without defensiveness, sparking sudden insights and giving them room to grow into new understanding.

As different perspectives emerge, the thinking of both mentor and mentee expand. For example, a mentee might ask his mentor, "What do you think are the most important qualities in a good leader?"

Instead of listing qualities, the mentor throws the question back. "Well, who was a leader who made a difference in your life or resonated for you?"

Once the mentee offers examples of the leaders in his life, the mentor might ask, "What were the qualities of those leaders that made a personal difference?"

As they explore different qualities, the mentor realizes that his mentee represents a younger demographic and sees things somewhat differently. He shares his perceptions and asks the mentee about those differences. Together they come to a new understanding. The mentor says, "I have learned something new from you about how a younger demographic looks to leaders. That is going to be important for me in my own role and different from what I usually focus on." The mentee has gained a new perspective as well. Both parties will have expanded their understanding through dialogue.

Strategies for Good Conversation

It sounds straightforward—ask open-ended questions, listen actively to what your mentee is saying, and clarify understanding to make sure you are both on the same page. But as all experienced mentors know, staying in authentic conversation throughout a mentoring relationship can be challenging. You will need to think and work your way into good conversation. It's easy to fall back on sharing wisdom, giving advice, and answering questions. But as the Levels of Conversation Model (Figure 10.1) makes clear, the real work of conversation is not handing over a to-do list or book of personal aphorisms, but building trust with your mentees and encouraging them to grow and develop into their own authentic selves. Mentoring conversations, with work and discipline, can help us connect with one another at the deepest level and bring us to new places of insight. Maximize your mentoring time and experience by understanding the elements of a productive conversation and knowing how to put them into action.

Ask Open-Ended Questions

A mentor's thought-provoking questions can pave the way to a mentee's self-discovery and insight, and the ability to ask the right questions is an extremely important mentoring skill. It allows you to facilitate and deepen your mentee's learning and helps you establish a meaningful connection with the other person. Knowing how to use questions to facilitate mentee learning is art as well as science.

The art of asking questions involves knowing how to:

- Ask questions that tap into a mentee's unique experiences.
- Ask questions that challenge a mentee's intellect while also being sensitive to her feelings and comfort level.
- Ask questions that draw on the strength of the mentee's learning style, while at the same time being sensitive to unique cultural differences.
- Stage questions in such a way that they cascade and build on one another to lead the mentee to deeper insights.

The science is in knowing what kind of questions to ask:

- Good questions are clear, relevant, and specific.
- Good questions must relate to a mentee's real-world issues and concerns.
- Good questions are open-ended, requiring more than a simple yes or no response.
- Good questions should encourage personal reflection on past experiences and facilitate the self-discovery of answers.
- Good questions must always be asked with genuine curiosity about the answers.

Listen Actively

Active listening, and making sure you understand your mentee's response, is the other half of the questioning equation. Conversations are enriched by the depth and breadth of the mentor's questions, but it is virtually impossible to ask the appropriate questions if you are not actively listening to your mentee.

Strategies for Listening Actively

Active listening includes these basic elements:

- Set the stage for active listening: Remove distractions and interruptions during mentoring meetings. Don't answer calls, check email, or do other tasks while you are engaged in conversation with your mentee. Multitasking and other interruptions are a sign that your mentoring partner is not as important as your personal agenda.

- Pay attention: Give your mentoring partner's words your full attention rather than thinking about what you want to say while he is still talking. Show you are listening by giving nonverbal cues—nod your head in agreement, smile, make good eye contact.

- Clarify: Restating what you heard for clarification ("So, you're saying that . . .") reinforces listening and avoids making assumptions. Probing for more with open-ended questions ("What made you feel that way?") also demonstrates that you are listening.

- Acknowledge feelings: Don't be afraid to acknowledge strong feelings when you hear them ("It sounds like you were really frustrated"). This is another way to show that you are listening, and it helps you better understand what is really going on. Pay attention to hesitancy or pausing—clues that something is not being said—and probe further, if appropriate ("I'm wondering why that bothered you so much . . .").

After your mentoring conversation, take a moment to think about how well you listened and what you can do better. Practice your listening skills in a variety of settings—staff meetings, and meetings with direct reports.

Listening Actively During Virtual Conversations

You will probably find yourself engaging in virtual conversation during your mentoring relationship. Geographic differences make it imperative to rely on email, Skype, videoconferencing, FaceTime, virtual mentoring platforms, and the like. Each offers efficient and convenient ways to connect but also presents potential challenges, even to the most adept listeners.

As with all conversation—whether across the desk, the phone, or the Internet—what you communicate is not always what you meant to say. No matter what form of communication you use for mentoring conversations, remember to check out your assumptions. You will also want to assess how well the technology is helping or getting in the way, and whether it is creating misunderstandings.

Agree in advance

Discuss which modes of communication will work for both you and your mentoring partner. Base your selection on what has the greatest likelihood of facilitating good conversation, not just which is easiest and most convenient. Experiment with multiple modalities to see what works best for you. Maintain focus by agreeing to minimize distractions and interruptions. And keep checking in periodically to ensure that communication is effective.

Don't rely on email and texting as a substitute for real conversation.

Optimize telephone conversations

Visual cues and body language are the most reliable means of effective communication. Without them, it is easy to misinterpret intended meaning. Because telephone conversations are dependent on voice tone, they lack this vital visual information. This means that the listener needs to work harder at listening. Verify your understanding of what you heard. Provide clear verbal clues to your partner that you are tuned in (you might, for example, say "Uh-huh, I see," and so on to let your partner know that you are actively listening).

Ask for clarification

Let your partner know what you are doing if it is going to prevent you from actively listening. If, for example, you are capturing a note, idea, action, or recommendation, ask your partner to give you a moment because you are writing or typing. Don't multitask, and don't interrupt.

Use email effectively

Email is the best way to confirm appointments, provide updates, and forward agendas, articles, or summaries for future discussion. It is not an optimum way to communicate more deeply.

- Email lacks tonality. Because it requires interpretation of meaning, there is always a high risk that at some point there will be a misunderstanding. A remark intended to be humorous can easily be interpreted as serious—and even insulting.

- Avoid this situation by communicating sensitive information, particularly feedback and critical conversations, using other means—in person, by Skype or FaceTime, or over the phone. When you receive an emotional or confusing email, stop—resist the temptation to react immediately, and before you respond, ask for clarification.

- *Don't* rely on email when there is a high likelihood of emotion and potential for misinterpretation.

Use Skype and FaceTime effectively

Virtual communication has the advantage of simulating real-time interaction, but it also has its challenges, not the least of which are technology glitches. Although Skype and FaceTime offer the advantage of facial expression and voice to communicate meaning in real time, body language—a critical element—is often missed. Ensure that you make eye contact with one another if you are taking notes. *Don't* use up precious conversation time trying to repair technology problems. Create a Plan B for dealing with technology problems.

Clarify Understanding

"We see the world, not as it is, but as we are." Anais Nin's famous observation reminds us that what we hear, read, or see is filtered by our unique views of the world. It is natural for us to interpret what we hear through our own filters. This is why is essential to take the time to clarify what your mentee is saying. It will give you a more accurate read on where your mentee is really coming from. Clarifying has the added benefit of validating important insights and demonstrating that you are listening actively.

Clarifying understanding can be accomplished easily by applying some time-tested techniques:

- Test your understanding by asking questions and getting confirmation. "Are you saying . . .?" "Did you mean . . .?" "So it sounds like you feel . . ."

- Paraphrase. Rephrase (shorter and clearer) what you heard your mentee say. Make sure your mentee confirms your interpretation before moving forward.

  "I hear you saying . . . Is that what you meant?"

- Ask for definitions or meaning.

  "What do you mean when you say 'rigid'?" Or "How do you define 'rigid'?"

- Offer an interpretation.

  "When you say 'rigid,' do you mean . . .?" This is useful if your mentee is struggling to put something into words. Again, get confirmation before moving forward.

- Highlight a major insight.

  "So, you're coming to realize that . . .? That's a great insight."

While clarifying understanding is essential, take care to avoid some common pitfalls. For example, don't assume you know what your mentee means. Avoid making statements that negate the mentee's point of view. Take care not alter your mentee's ideas or points of view when you paraphrase her words. Don't allow significant mentee comments or insights to pass without addressing them.

Six Essential Mentoring Conversations

You and your mentee will have many conversations over the course of your mentoring partnership. When you enter into conversation consciously, with specific goals in mind, you can use these conversations to build the trust, boundaries, and goals that allow the relationship to grow and thrive.

The six mentoring conversations in this section are essential during the first ninety days of a mentoring relationship. You'll read about each conversation and its challenges, strategies for success, and some probing questions you can use to engage your mentee in conversation. As Cynthia and Rafa's story demonstrates, these conversations won't necessarily take place in successive mentoring meetings. They may unfold in this order, but not necessarily meeting by meeting. For example, with some mentees you may progress quickly, covering the first two conversations in the first meeting; with others it may take several meetings to create a safe space in which you can both move forward.

Conversation 1. Building a Relationship

New mentees are often uncertain and cautious, reluctant to reveal their struggles to someone in a position to influence their career success. It is only when they establish an authentic, meaningful, trusting relationship with their mentor that they feel comfortable enough to lower their guard and become open to learning. Working on building a trusting relationship with a mentee should be your first conversation.

You might be tempted to skip over relationship-building conversations, particularly if you have had prior experience working with your mentee and feel that you already know them. Or, pressed for time, you may simply decide you both need to get down to business and start working. We cannot stress enough the importance of intentionally establishing a groundwork of trust with your mentee. Without trust, there will be no real relationship.

Relationship building is not a one-time task, but rather an ongoing aspect of mentoring conversation. Each rich, honest, personal, and real conversation strengthens trust and deepens the relationship. Depending on a variety of factors (past history with each other, organizational culture, personal compatibility, reputation, personality, or propensity to trust), you may find that you need to engage in several conversations before you have developed a solid foundation of trust.

Not every mentor is comfortable with or adept at relationship building. It is easy to get frustrated, because it takes time and may not produce immediate results. However, we know that if you invest the time in the beginning to build a trusting relationship with your mentee, it will create a solid foundation that will enhance the learning that follows.

Strategies for Success

1. Review information about your mentoring partner (bio/resume/CV) before your first meeting so you can identify potential areas of commonality and mutual interest.

2. Ensure privacy and a lack of interruption and distraction by scheduling meetings away from your office, if possible.

3. Ask your mentee about the people who have influenced him the most in his career. Be prepared to talk about your own mentors and the people who influenced you.

4. Share stories about your own career journey. Set the stage for open, honest conversation by being authentic about your struggles as well as your successes.

5. Discuss your mutual learning styles, personality traits, Myers-Briggs profiles, or other assessment results that will give you additional insights about each other.

6. Explore your mentee's career motivations and what drives him before you move on.

Probing Questions

- Why did you choose your current career path?
- How do you (did you) deal with adversity?
- How do you let off steam?
- What do you like best about yourself?
- What has been a key leadership lesson for you?
- How do you spend your free time?
- Why did you choose me as your mentor?
- How do you think I can best help you?

Are You Ready for Conversation 2?

When you and your mentoring partner have reached a comfortable level of connection—your mentee is speaking up, asking questions, and seems willing to talk about career challenges—you're ready to move on. Your next step is to establish agreements that frame the work of your mentoring relationship.

Conversation 2. Establishing Mentoring Agreements

As a rule, most mentoring partners don't take enough time to set up relationship agreements and ground rules. (Informal mentoring relationships often bypass this process altogether.) Just as trust helps establish a real relationship, taking the time to lay out a structure for your relationship makes a big difference in navigating your relationship, focusing the learning, and staying on track.

Everyone holds different understandings, assumptions, and expectations about mentoring. For example, you might assume that your mentee is a novice with little expertise and experience and will be looking to you for information and answers. Your mentee, on the other hand, may be looking for something altogether different—a safe place to share thinking, explore ideas, and get your validation. Having a conversation about assumptions helps avoid disappointment and conflict later on. And even though it may be uncomfortable to talk about, expectations about confidentiality should be explored at the start of the mentoring relationship as well.

By discussing concerns, limitations, hot buttons, and personal boundaries up front, mentors and mentees can start off on the right foot and avoid unintentionally derailing the relationship. Even something as obvious as logistics need to be negotiated— where, when, and how to meet are part of agreements you will need to determine together.

Strategies for Success

1. Make sure you and your mentoring partner talk about the assumptions you hold about your roles as mentor and mentee and what you each expect from the other. Convert your understanding into agreements. (For example, while your mentee may want answers from you, your role is to help her find her own.)

2. Discuss the role of confidentiality in the relationship and why it is important. Share your mutual expectations and understanding of what it means and how it might play out in your relationship.

3. Talk about how to best use your time. Determine what kind of preparation you might need in advance of meetings. (For example, some mentoring partners have the mentee

formulate an agenda in advance of the meeting, with topics for discussion.)

4. Talk about your hot buttons—things that get in the way and annoy you. (For example, your mentee may get irritated if you don't arrive precisely on time, while your idea of "on time" means it's permissible to be up to ten minutes late.)

5. Set ground rules for your relationship. Create agreements that will help you improve your interactions with each other and keep you both on track. (For example, no phone calls during meetings; come prepared; if a meeting must be cancelled, reschedule immediately.)

6. Agree to set up two-way feedback and check-in conversations to assess satisfaction with progress, relationship, and learning. Schedule them in advance on your calendar.

Probing Questions

- What does confidentiality mean to you?
- How often do you see us meeting?
- Where is a comfortable place for us to meet?
- How can we ensure that we stay on track and are productive?
- What kind of preparation would help us?
- What hot buttons do you have that might impact our relationship?
- Can you think of any other parameters we need to discuss?

Are You Ready for Conversation 3?

Once you and your mentoring partner have established clear agreements, go ahead and roll up your sleeves: your learning journey is about to begin. The next conversation focuses on goal setting and identifying the areas on which the learning will focus.

Conversation 3. Moving from Starter Goals to Smarter Goals

Mentoring relationships are innately goal-centered. Goals focus the work of mentoring, enable mentee growth and development, and ultimately determine the success of the relationship. They are indispensable to the work of mentoring. Setting SMART— specific, measurable, action-oriented, realistic, and timely—learning goals is one of the most daunting challenges mentors and mentees face. This is why the goal-setting conversations are as important as arriving at the goals themselves.

Although both mentor and mentee must play active roles in the goal-setting process, the mentor is responsible for facilitating the process of setting goals. The mentor's role is to ensure that the mentee's goals fit within the framework of workplace reality, tap into the mentee's capability and talent, and also help stretch their competency and capability.

Mentees are often reluctant to identify goals that might appear too ambitious to a senior leader. Mentees may secretly think, "I want your job," but fear getting feedback from their mentor that signals they lack the talent or skills to get there. In a desire to look good in front of their mentor, or to avoid stumbling, mentees can select goals that are too easily accomplished. Some mentees mistake tasks for goals and formulate a "to do" list rather than a "to learn" list. Without input from assessments or surveys, or candid feedback from their supervisor, some mentees simply don't know where they stand and where they need to focus their energies.

Mentors can also feel pressured by the goal-setting process. Some see their mentee's goal accomplishment as a reflection of their own competency; others feel a weight of responsibility for producing goals with tangible results. Some organizations want assurances that the mentee's goals will measure up to the mentoring investment. Your ability to identify growth goals that will make a meaningful contribution to this person's success warrants the work and effort.

Strategies for Success

1. Ask questions to stimulate discussion about your mentee's motivations and aspirations.

2. Have your mentee describe himself five years from now. Get him to be specific about what he is doing, skills he is using, and challenges he is taking on.

3. Encourage your mentee to get feedback from others, including peers, direct reports, and supervisors.

4. Arrange for your mentee to meet with successful, admired leaders to help discern what skills, talents, attributes, and characteristics were important to their success.

5. Help your mentee identify assignments, challenges, and tasks that push him out of his comfort zone, and areas where he needs to gain confidence and competence. Set goals in those areas.

6. Ask the "why" question for each potential goal. Why is this goal important to your development?

Probing Questions

- Where do you see yourself in five years?
- What would your ideal day look like five years from now?
- What do you see as your strengths and challenges?
- What skills and talents are you underutilizing?
- How can you make a bigger impact?
- What are some of the problems and challenges you are currently facing?

- What is holding you back?
- When was the last time you felt fully energized and engaged at work? What were you doing?

Are You Ready for Conversation 4?

You'll know you're ready for Conversation 4 when both mentor and mentee are enthusiastic and energized by the goals you've identified together and you are confident that achieving these can positively impact the mentee's growth and development. Now you can both begin to create a work plan for achieving the goals you've mutually agreed on. Together, determine what kinds of learning opportunities might help your mentee accomplish his goals.

Conversation 4. Creating Learning Opportunities

One of the best ways to keep a mentoring relationship fresh is to build in multiple learning opportunities. Learning opportunities should lead to behavioral, attitudinal, and/or skill changes that will make a significant difference to the mentee's success.

Mentees tell us that some of their biggest gains have come from being pushed out of their comfort zone and "forced" to try something new. Reading an article or book is not transforming in itself, but if that reading sparks a new way of thinking and prompts experimentation and risk taking, it is valuable. Tasks like interviewing a leader or writing an article are a good start on a goal, but they are not sufficient in and of themselves. If a mentee can accomplish this too easily, the learning opportunity won't push her development forward.

Learning opportunities should be challenging, requiring mentees to stretch. Just moving out of their comfort zone and trying something new can be empowering. They end up feeling more confident, competent, and comfortable as a result, and—ideally—they've learned something new about themselves.

Perhaps your mentee could benefit by exposure to additional knowledge, skills, and experience. Reach out to colleagues and professional networks to find out what kinds of learning opportunities others have had or could make available to your mentee. Brainstorm a list of learning opportunities together with your mentee. As you do, think about learning style, context, goals, and timing.

Strategies for Success

1. Ask the mentee to identify activities and opportunities that would stretch her to grow and develop. Don't be surprised if your mentee comes up with ideas you've never considered.
2. Ask the mentee about activities and behaviors that take her out of her comfort zone.
3. Identify ways to expand the mentee's current knowledge and understanding.
4. Before beginning a stretch project, help your mentee address her concerns, challenges, and issues so she feels more comfortable and prepared.
5. Ask the mentee how you can best support him as he engages in new learning.
6. Create a schedule for checking in: assessing progress, getting feedback and identifying lessons learned while she is pursuing her learning opportunities.

Probing Questions

- When was the last time you pushed yourself out of your comfort zone?
- What would it take to get you out of your comfort zone?
- What is something you've been afraid to try that would challenge you?

- What additional knowledge, skill, or experience are you lacking?
- What can I do to support you in your learning right now?

Are You Ready for Conversation 5?

Many mentees (and mentors) struggle as they tackle their learning goals. While the mentee is accountable for working on his goal, your role as a mentor is to be supportive. Ask stimulating, reflective questions to help him integrate his learning and contribute to his growth. Help him move closer to his future vision of himself once he has accomplished his goal. Learning opportunities should include challenges that will stretch the mentee and take him out of his comfort zone, expose him to new learning, and accelerate and reinforce learning.

As your mentee pushes past his comfort zone, your mentoring relationship may encounter stumbling blocks. These obstacles are inevitable, and it's important to be ready to manage them when they come up.

Conversation 5. Managing Stumbling Blocks

Stumbling blocks commonly occur once a mentee takes on a development goal, faces a new challenge, or is pushed out of her comfort zone. Problems may be compounded as mentees struggle with balancing their workload along with their commitment to their own growth and development.

Be on the lookout for symptoms that your mentee is having a problem: Mentoring meetings get cancelled and are not rescheduled. Conversations become transactional. The mentee comes to a meeting unprepared or fails to follow through on a commitment. The energy level of one or both mentoring partners is low.

There doesn't seem to be anything substantial to talk about when you get together. Enthusiasm wanes.

It is far easier to deal with stumbling blocks if you and your mentee have previously agreed on how to address them if they surface. In any case, it is important for the success of the relationship to address stumbling blocks as soon as they arise.

Strategies for Success

1. Make sure you have a mutually agreed-on process in place to address stumbling blocks *before* they occur.

2. Pay attention to your hunches, intuition, and feelings. When something seems wrong, check it out.

3. Don't leave too long a gap between meetings. Lulls often lead to permanent inertia.

4. Provide positive and constructive feedback on a regular basis.

5. Consider how you might be contributing to the problem. (Have you held your mentee accountable, pushed her out of her comfort zone, or provided timely, candid feedback? If not, your mentee may have opted to focus on other priorities for which she is being held accountable for results.)

6. Focus on fixing the problem rather than being defensive.

Probing Questions

- Lately, we seem to be struggling to meet. What do you think is getting in the way?

- We don't seem to have a clear focus of conversation. How can we turn that around?

- I sense you are struggling with follow-through on your mentoring commitments. Do you feel that way too?

- Our mentoring meetings always seem to focus on your current crisis. Is that the most productive use of our time?

- I feel like we keep rewinding the tape of the same conversation and not making forward progress. Is that your take as well?

- You agreed three weeks ago that you would send me two or three potential goals you want to work on, but I haven't received them yet. What's up?

- I feel less energy from you than when we first started meeting. Is that your observation too? What do you think is contributing to that?

Are You Ready for Conversation 6?

In the stumbling block conversation, the mentor and mentee address existing or potential problems. When you both feel that you have moved past the stumbling block, the course of mentoring can continue. At some point, you will want to check in together to touch base on progress.

The check-in conversation is different from the stumbling block conversation: it is designed to identify each partner's areas of satisfaction and learning. You can avoid future problems by taking the time to examine ways to improve the mentoring experience for both of you.

Conversation 6. Checking In on Progress

There is nothing like progress to fuel a mentoring relationship. When partners feel their investment is paying off with new learning, growth, and insights, the mentoring relationship thrives. Staying on track will help ensure that you reap the full benefit of your mentoring experience.

Staying on track means paying attention to three areas: the relationship, the learning process, and progress on goals. Don't assume that you and your mentoring partner experience all three areas in the same way. A check-in conversation, scheduled at a predetermined milestone (for example, three months), will ensure that you and your mentee are on the same page before moving forward.

Use a check-in to identify areas of satisfaction for each partner, and your mentee's key insights to date. Share what you are learning from the relationship. Allocate time to review the mentee's goals, strategies, and work plan, and check for his level of satisfaction. Probe for any issues that have not yet surfaced. Even if both parties are satisfied, brainstorm ways to improve the mentoring experience.

Strategies for Success

1. Talk about the value of a check-in conversation early in the process. Schedule dates on the calendar to ensure adequate preparation.

2. Start on a positive note by identifying what you find particularly satisfying.

3. Discuss format, length, location, preparation, and planning of mentoring meetings to ensure these are working for both partners.

4. Discuss the learning process to date.

5. Ask your mentee to share examples of the kind of support he values and finds helpful.

6. Evaluate the learning opportunities and challenges that are currently in place.

Probing Questions

- What have you learned from this experience thus far?
- What are some of your biggest insights and aha's?
- What are you doing differently now as a result of the mentoring relationship?

- What more can I do to help support you?

- What more can I do to help stimulate your learning, reflection, and thinking?

- Are you getting out of your comfort zone and stretching yourself? What more can you do? How can I help?

- Are we moving fast enough? Do we need to slow things down?

Afterword: Starting Strong, Moving Forward

Our goal in writing this book was to combine the power of story with the power of practice. We wanted to invite you directly into the rarely observed mentoring conversations that take place during the first ninety days of a mentoring relationship—to give you a touch, a taste, and a feel for the dilemmas, emotions, and thinking of both mentor and mentee.

Cynthia and Rafa needed to start strong, to work on their relationship before they moved forward. They needed time and continued good conversation to create mutual trust so they could be authentic with one another. And, as Rafa learned, it was the goal conversation, rather than the goal itself, that elevated the quality of the mentoring partnership. We hope that you will be engaging in similar conversations during your first ninety days.

Our clients are always asking for the "toolkit" that will enable them to start strong and keep the conversations going. In this book, we hope that we've given you not only a good story, but a solid framework and tools that will help you elevate your own mentoring conversations. If nothing else, we hope that *Starting Strong* has compelled you to think about your own mentoring practice and to take your mentoring to the next level.

Suggested Reading

Covey, S. *The 7 Habits of Highly Effective People*. New York: Simon & Schuster, 1989.

Heath, C., and Heath, D. *Switch: How to Change Things When Change Is Hard*. New York: Broadway Books, 2010.

Lencioni, P. *The Five Dysfunctions of a Team*. San Francisco: Jossey-Bass, 2002.

Lewis, M. *Moneyball: The Art of Winning an Unfair Game*. New York: Norton, 2004.

Luft, J., and Ingham, H. *The Johari Window, A Graphic Model of Interpersonal Awareness*. Proceedings of the Western Training Laboratory in Group Development. Los Angeles: UCLA, 1955.

Zachary, L. J. *The Mentor's Guide: Facilitating Effective Learning Relationships*. San Francisco: Jossey-Bass, 2011.

Zachary, L. J. *Creating a Mentoring Culture: The Organization's Guide*. San Francisco: Jossey-Bass, 2005.

Zachary, L. J., and Fischler, L. A. *The Mentee's Guide: Making Mentoring Work for You*. San Francisco: Jossey-Bass, 2009.

Acknowledgments

The mark of a really good partnership is to continue to learn from and be inspired by each other—to appreciate each other's gifts and talents, and to grow from the experience of collaboration. We thank each other, and once again celebrate our collaboration and friendship.

But in truth, we did not go it alone. In writing this book, there were many people who supported and inspired us:

Our husbands, Ed Zachary and Ron Fischler, who have always been steadfast in their support and have come to love Rafa and Cynthia almost as much as we do

David Brightman, senior editor at Jossey-Bass, and Sheryl Fullerton, former executive editor, whose encouragement and support know no bounds

Naomi Lucks, development editor, our very talented and creative partner, who kept us on track with her probing questions, gentle nudges, and lighthearted humor

And especially the many mentees, mentors, and program managers who candidly shared their mentoring stories, successes, and struggles from their first ninety days

About the Authors

Lois J. Zachary is an internationally recognized expert on mentoring. She has been cited as "one of the top one hundred minds in leadership" today. Her book *The Mentor's Guide*, first published in 2000 and revised in 2012, is the primary resource for organizations interested in promoting mentoring for leadership and learning and for mentors seeking to deepen their mentoring practice. With her bestselling books *Creating a Mentoring Culture* (2005), *The Mentee's Guide: Making Mentoring Work for You* (Jossey-Bass, 2009, with coauthor Lory Fischler), and *The Mentor's Guide*, five Mentoring Excellence Pocket Toolkits, and over one hundred published articles, Dr. Zachary has created a comprehensive set of resources for facilitating the practice of individual and organizational mentoring excellence. Her most recently published book, *My Mother Has the Finest Eyes*, is a collection of poetry and reflection.

Dr. Zachary is president of Leadership Development Services, LLC, a Phoenix-based consulting firm that specializes in leadership and mentoring, and director of its Center for Mentoring Excellence. Her innovative mentoring approaches and expertise in coaching leaders and their organizations in designing, implementing, and evaluating learner-centered mentoring programs have been used globally by a wide array of clients, including

Fortune 100 companies, government organizations, and educational and other institutions, both profit and nonprofit.

Lory Fischler is a senior associate with Leadership Development Services, LLC, and associate director of its Center for Mentoring Excellence. She is a dynamic, insightful, and seasoned professional with over twenty-five years' experience in consulting, training, and coaching clients from a diverse array of organizations, including Fortune 500, health care, manufacturing, government, and nonprofit.

Fischler is the coauthor, with Lois J. Zachary, of *The Mentee's Guide* and the Mentoring Excellence Pocket Toolkits, and has published a number of articles. She is the creator of Leadership Development Services' Workstyle Inventory, a tool widely used by clients to promote self-understanding and team interaction, and the designer and facilitator of Negotiating: Win-Win Results, a three-day experiential workshop that has been delivered worldwide.

Index

Page references followed by *fig* indicate an illustrated figure.